A Writing Process Book

interactions two

A Writing Process Book

interactions two

Third Edition

Margaret Keenan Segal

Cheryl Pavlik

With contributions by Laurie Blass

The McGraw-Hill Companies, Inc.

New York St. Louis San Francisco Auckland Bogotá Caracas Lisbon
London Madrid Mexico City Milan Montreal New Delhi San Juan
Singapore Sydney Tokyo Toronto

This is an  book.

McGraw-Hill

A Division of The McGraw·Hill Companies

Interactions Two
A Writing Process Book
Third Edition

2 3 4 5 6 7 8 9 0   DOC   DOC   9 0 9 8 7

ISBN 0-07-057103-1
ISBN 0-07-114374-2

This book was set in Times Roman by Clarinda.

The editors were Tim Stookesberry, Bill Preston, and Julia Falsetti; the designers were
Lorna Lo, Suzanne Montazer, Francis Owens, and Elizabeth Williamson; the production
supervisor was Phyllis Snyder; the project editor was Stacey Sawyer; the cover was
designed by Francis Owens; the cover illustrator was Mark Chickinelli; the photo researcher
was Cindy Robinson, Seaside Publishing; illustrations were done by David Bohn, Axelle
Fortier, Rick Hackney, Lori Heckelman, and Sally Richardson.

R. R. Donnelley & Sons Company, Crawfordsville, IN was printer and binder.
Phoenix Color Corporation was cover separator and printer.

Library of Congress Catalog Card Number: 96-75161.

Photo credits:

Page 1 © Beringer / The Image Works; *2* © Chistopher Briscoe / Photo Researchers, Inc.; *3* ©
Joseph Schuyler / Stock, Boston; *6* © Jeff Greenberg / Photo Researchers, Inc.; *7* © Deni
McIntyre; *12* © Alan Karey / The Image Works; *14* © John Fung; *17* © John Fung; *18 (top)* ©
Barbara Rios / Photo Researchers, Inc.; *18 (bottom)* © Katherine McGlynn / The Image Works;
22 © Renate Hiller / Monkmeyer Press; *24* © Bill Anderson / Monkmeyer Press; *29* © Katrina
Thomas / Photo Researchers, Inc.; *31* © John Fung; *35* © Peter Menzel / Stock, Boston;

continued on page 222

Contents

Preface
to the Third Edition
The Interactions Two Program

The Interactions Two program consists of five texts and a variety of supplemental materials for low-intermediate to intermediate students seeking to improve their English language skills. Each of the five texts in this program is carefully organized by chapter theme, vocabulary, grammar structures, and, where possible, language functions. As a result, information introduced in a chapter of any one of the Interactions Two texts corresponds to and reinforces material taught in the same chapter of the other four books, creating a truly integrated, four-skills approach.

The Interactions Two program is highly flexible. The texts in this series may be used together or separately, depending on students' needs and course goals. The books in this program include:

- **A Communicative Grammar Book.** Organized around grammatical topics, this book includes notional/functional material where appropriate. It presents all grammar in context and contains many types of communicative activities.
- **A Listening/Speaking Skills Book.** This book uses lively, natural language from various contexts, including dialogues, interviews, lectures, and announcements. Listening strategies emphasized include summarizing main ideas, making inferences, listening for stressed words, reductions and intonation. A variety of speaking activities complement the listening component.
- **A Reading Skills Book.** The reading selections contain sophisticated college-level material; however, vocabulary and grammar have been carefully controlled to be at students' level of comprehension. The text includes many vocabulary-building exercises and emphasizes reading strategies such as skimming, scanning, guessing meaning from context, understanding the structure and organization of a selection, increasing reading speed, and interpreting the author's point of view.
- **A Writing Process Book.** This book uses a process approach to writing, including many exercises on prewriting and revision. Exercises build skills in exploring and organizing ideas; developing vocabulary; using correct form and mechanics; using coherent structure, and editing, revising, and using feedback to create a final draft.
- **A Multi-Skills Activity Book.** New to this edition, this text gives students integrated practice in all four language skills. Among the communicative activities included in this text are exercises for the new video program that accompanies the Interactions Two series.

Supplemental Materials

In addition to the five core texts outlined above, various supplemental materials are available to assist users of the third edition, including:

Instructor's Manual

Extensively revised for the new edition, this manual provides instructions and guidelines for using the five core texts separately or in various combinations to suit particular program needs. For each of the core texts, there is a separate section with answer keys, teaching tips, additional activities, and other suggestions. The testing materials have been greatly expanded in this edition.

Audio Program for *Interactions Two: A Listening/Speaking Skills Book*

Completely re-recorded for the new edition, the audio program is designed to be used in conjunction with those exercises that are indicated with a cassette icon in the student text. Complete tapescripts are now included in the back of the student text.

Audio Program to Accompany *Interactions Two: A Reading Skills Book*

This new optional audio program contains selected readings from the student text. These taped selections enable students to listen at their leisure to the natural oral discourse of native readers for intonation and modeling. Readings that are included in this program are indicated with a cassette icon in the student text.

Video

New to this edition, the video program for Interactions Two contains authentic television segments that are coordinated with the twelve chapter themes in the five texts. Exercises and activities for this video are in the Multi-Skills Activity Book.

Interactions Two: A Writing Process Book, Third Edition

Interactions Two: A Writing Process Book, Third Edition, was designed to lead students through the writing process and provide an assortment of activities to help them master the wide array of writing skills necessary for good writing. Each of the twelve chapters in this text is divided into a number of distinct sections focusing on different steps in the writing process. These sections introduce various writing strategies and techniques and allow students to practice them one step at a time. This practice helps students understand how the different techniques work before they use them in their own writing. Students are given specific guidance in using their new skills to generate and organize ideas and to write, edit, and revise paragraphs of their own. At every step, students are encouraged to analyze and discuss the strategies they are using: In this way, students focus on one skill at a time. Beginning students especially benefit from this step-by-step approach because they are usually more comfortable with structured practice. By the end of each chapter, the students will have acquired new skills and produced their own paragraphs.

Special appendixes at the end of the book provide spelling, punctuation, and capitalization rules that students can use for reference. There are also feedback sheets for the instructor's use (see Teaching Suggestions, page ix).

Although the concept of writing as a process is central to the course, traditional areas of instruction such as paragraph form, mechanics, and grammar are practiced throughout. The emphasis, however, is on grammatical and lexical features that serve to unify a paragraph.

Our own classroom experience shows that the analysis of model paragraphs can be helpful and instructive. Therefore, the chapters also contain two or three tasks based on model paragraphs.

Chapter Organization

1. **Exploring Ideas.** The first problem that most students encounter is a difficulty in generating ideas. This section teaches strategies to help them with that task. Some of the methods presented are discussing and listing ideas, interviewing, and free writing. A vocabulary-building activity gives students some of the language they may need in writing their own paragraphs and encourages them to use fellow students and their teachers as resources for additional vocabulary development.

2. **Organizing Ideas.** In this section, students are taught organizational skills such as writing effective topic sentences, limiting the information in a paragraph, and organizing different types of paragraphs.

3. **Developing Cohesion and Style.** This section focuses on the grammatical and lexical features that unify a paragraph. Students are taught the most natural use of structures and vocabulary in extended written discourse. Some sentence-level structures that often cause students problems, such as choice of tense, are also covered in this section.

4. **Writing the First Draft.** Because most students do not realize that good writing is usually the product of many revisions, they are explicitly told that the first paragraph they write is only a draft.

5. **Editing Practice.** One of the most important skills for students to master is the ability to edit their own work. This section gives them paragraphs that contain common errors of from, grammar, cohesion, and organization. By finding errors in compositions they have not written, students learn to critically evaluate their own work with less anxiety. A positive approach to this step is recommended. Students should not be expected to find all errors, and working in small groups can make this activity more fun.

6. **Editing Your Writing.** After students practice editing other paragraphs, they are asked to edit their own compositions. Teachers can ask students to focus on specific aspects of their writing to make this task less frustrating. We also suggest that students work with partners so they can help each other with this important step.

7. **Writing the Second Draft.** Only after students have had a chance to revise and edit their own compositions are they required to hand in neatly written papers for the teacher's evaluation.

A Step Beyond. Too often, students' interest in their writing ends once they receive a grade. This final section provides a variety of additional activities to encourage students to communicate with each other through their writing. Suggestions include using writing as the basis of debate or discussion, creating class books with student paragraphs, and displaying writing on bulletin boards. Unstructured journal writing assignments, both on and off the chapter topic, are also featured here for extra writing practice.

Teaching Suggestions

The text has been designed for four hours of classwork per chapter, with homework assignments after each class. Some groups may require more classroom time. Although the text provides a set format, it should not be considered prescriptive. More sophisticated students who may have already developed their own writing strategies should not be forced to abandon them. In addition, we recommend that you ask the students to do as much extra free writing as possible; the *Instructor's Manual* contains additional suggestions for assigning unstructured writing work.

Many activities in the text are described as group work and are denoted as such by the group icon. Although teachers should feel free to adapt the tasks according to the needs and abilities of their own students, we feel that group and pair work help students develop self-confidence. Because writing is such a daunting task for most students, working with others may help them see that all students have many of the same difficulties.

The feedback sheets at the end of the book help teachers organize their comments in a way that students can easily interpret. Teachers are encouraged to give as much positive feedback as possible, to focus on content before grammar, and to concentrate on those skills that are presented in each particular chapter. This practice is especially vital for beginning students, whose mistakes are so numerous.

New to the Third Edition

The third edition of *Interactions Two: A Writing Process Book* remains dedicated to providing students with a variety of activities that guide them through the process of writing. However, each chapter of the third edition includes many new features; here are the highlights:

1. **Streamlined Design.** The new edition features an attractive two-color design and an extensively revised art program. These changes were initiated to make the books more appealing, up-to-date, and user friendly. In addition, we made the books easier to use by simplifying complicated direction lines, numbering exercises and activities, and highlighting key information in shaded boxes and charts.

2. **Revised Chapter Organization.** We streamlined the chapter organization in the third edition by collapsing some of the writing process steps, creating an easy-to-follow seven-step sequence (see Chapter Organization, page ix).

3. **New Chapter Theme on The Global Village.** The new edition features an entirely new theme for Chapter Six: The Global Village. In addition, the theme for Chapter Nine has been broadened and renamed Discoveries to include new content.

4. **What Do You Think?** These new boxed features in each chapter encourage students to relate their personal experience to an aspect of the chapter theme and to develop their critical thinking skills. Many of these new features include communicative pair activities.

5. **Focus on Testing.** Also appearing in each chapter, these new boxed features provide useful tips to help students prepare for test-taking situations where they must write essays under time pressure.

6. **Skills Chart.** A chart summarizing the writing skills and activities for all twelve chapters follows the preface.

Acknowledgments

Our thanks to the following reviewers whose comments, both favorable and critical, were of great value in the development of the third edition of the Interactions/Mosaic series:

Jean Al-Sibai, University of North Carolina; Janet Alexander, Waterbury College; Roberta Alexander, San Diego City College; Julie Alpert, Santa Barbara City College; Anita Cook, Tidewater Community College; Anne Deal Beavers, Heald Business College; Larry Berking, Monroe Community College; Deborah Busch, Delaware County Community College; Patricia A. Card, Chaminade University of Honolulu; Josá A. Carmona, Hudson County Community College; Kathleen Carroll, Fontbonne College; Consuela Chase, Loyola University; Lee Chen, California State University; Karen Cheng, University of Malaya; Gaye Childress, University of North Texas; Maria Conforti, University of Colorado; Earsie A. de Feliz, Arkansas State University; Elizabeth Devlin-Foltz, Montgomery County Adult Education; Colleen Dick, San Francisco Institute of English; Marta Dmytrenko-Ahrabian, Wayne State University; Margo Duffy, Northeast Wisconsin Technical; Magali Duignan,

Augusta College; Janet Dyar, Meridian Community College; Anne Ediger, San Diego City College; D. Frangie, Wayne State University; Robert Geryk, Wayne State University; Jeanne Gibson, American Language Academy; Kathleen Walsh Greene, Rhode Island College; Myra Harada, San Diego Mesa College; Kristin Hathhorn, Eastern Washington University; Mary Herbert, University of California, Davis; Joyce Homick, Houston Community College; Catherine Hutcheson, Texas Christian University; Suzie Johnston, Tyler Junior College; Donna Kauffman, Radford University; Emmie Lim, Cypress College; Patricia Mascarenas, Monte Vista Community School; Mark Mattison, Donnelly College; Diane Peak, Choate Rosemary Hall; James Pedersen, Irvine Valley College; Linda Quillan, Arkansas State University; Marnie Ramker, University of Illinois; Joan Roberts, The Doane Stuart School; Doralee Robertson, Jacksonville University; Ellen Rosen, Fullerton College; Jean Sawyer, American Language Academy; Frances Schulze, College of San Mateo; Sherrie R. Sellers, Brigham Young University; Tess M. Shafer, Edmonds Community College; Heinz F. Tengler, Lado International College; Sara Tipton, Wayne State University; Karen R. Vallejo, Brigham Young University; Susan Williams, University of Central Florida; Mary Shepard Wong, El Camino College; Cindy Yoder, Eastern Mennonite College; Cheryl L. Youtsey, Loyola University; Miriam Zahler, Wayne State University; Maria Zien, English Center, Miami; Yongmin Zhu, Los Medanos College; Norma Zorilla, Fresno Pacific College.

Summary of Writing Skills and Activities

Chapter	Rhetorical Focus	Organizing Skills	Grammar Focus
one	argument	• order of importance of ideas • giving reasons	• transition words: *because, so therefore, in addition, also first of all, finally*
two	description (place)	• writing topic sentences • writing concluding sentences • adding details	• giving reasons with *since* • varying word order
three	letter to the editor	• organization of a persuasive letter	• modals *must, have to, should, ought to* • making general statements
four	autobiographical narration	• limiting information • writing concluding sentences	• making predictions • past vs. present perfect vs. present perfect continuous • demonstratives
five	narration	• analyzing narrative organization • using details	• past vs. past perfect tense
six	argument	• clustering	• correct parts of speech • relative clauses • specific information
seven	narration	• keeping to the subject • paragraphing	• verbal adjectives • gerunds • parallel constructions • *would* and *used to*

Editing Skills	Communicative Activities	Critical Thinking	Test Preparation Activities
• paragraph format • present tense	• debating • discussing advertisements	• ranking arguments	• editing for transition words
• run-on sentences • noncount nouns	• playing a guessing game	• classifying sense details	• brainstorming for ideas
• avoiding faulty reasoning • spelling • syllabification	• making a bulletin board • debating • writing responses to letters	• evaluating arguments for faulty reasoning	• supporting your opinion
• omitting unimportant details • capitalization	• interviewing • writing a recommendation	• implying qualities	• checking for correct tense
• omitting digressions • using correct verb tenses	• sharing anecdotes	• analyzing the moral of a story	• checking for chronological order
• punctuation of relative clauses	• interviewing an older person • making a time capsule	• defining terms	• diagramming ideas
• omitting irrelevent details	• interviewing • sharing stories	• distinguishing appropriate topics	• developing ideas

Summary of Writing Skills and Activities

Chapter	Rhetorical Focus	Organizing Skills	Grammar Focus
eight	comparison	• similarities and differences • writing topic sentences • analyzing organization	• comparting with *both, neither, while, in contrast, on the other hand*
nine	description (a planet)	• making comparisons • keeping information together	• passive voice • giving reasons with *because* and *because of*
ten	argument	• focussing on a topic • supporting an argument with examples	• restrictive relative clauses • quotes • generalizations
eleven	newspaper article	• adding a title • organizing with questions	• relative clauses (review)
twelve	argument	• determining your audience • countering objections • making an outline	• conditional mood • review of transition words and logical connectors

Editing Skills	Communicative Activities	Critical Thinking	Test Preparation Activities
• gerunds • comparatives and superlatives	• discussing comparisons	• finding a basis of comparison	• listing ideas for comparison
• passive voice	• debating	• speculating	• making comparisons interesting
• using *the*	• debating • taking the opposite point of view	• distinguishing provable statements	• using quotations
• punctuating relative clauses	• making a class newspaper	• distinguishing fact from opinion	• checking for mechanics
• using correct connectors	• making a speech	• determining realistic solutions	• making an outline

CHAPTER one

Education and Student Life

You will write about the advantages of a large or small college.

Ranking Arguments

When you write a paragraph giving your opinion on a topic, it is important to rank your arguments in order of importance. This helps persuade the reader to see your point of view.

Here are some reasons an immigrant or international student might choose a college. Which ones are most important to you? Number them in order from 1 to 10, with 1 as the most important.

_____ class size

_____ facilities (libraries, laboratories)

_____ quality of ESL classes

_____ special programs for nonnative speakers

_____ courses offered

_____ location

_____ cost

_____ ease of admission

_____ prestige

_____ help with job placement

STEPS TO writing

1. Exploring Ideas
Choosing a College

A small suburban college

 **exercise** **1**   Think about the list of reasons in the What Do You Think box. What other reasons do you think are important to consider in choosing a college? List them on the lines below.

_____   _____

_____   _____

exercise 2   In small groups, discuss your ideas with other students. Tell why you thought certain reasons were important.

Lecture hall in a large college

Building Vocabulary

exercise 3   In your discussion about choosing a college you may have heard some words you don't understand, or you may have found that you didn't know the English words for some of the ideas you wanted to express. Ask the teacher the meaning of any words you don't understand and add them to the list below.

NOUNS	VERBS	ADJECTIVES	OTHER
advantage	attend	_____	_____
disadvantage	prefer	_____	_____
facility	_____	_____	_____
faculty	_____	_____	_____
location	_____	_____	_____
prestige	_____	_____	_____
_____	_____	_____	_____

exercise 4

In small groups, discuss the advantages of large and small colleges. Consider some of the things in the What Do You Think? box on page 2. Write your ideas on the lines below.

ADVANTAGES OF A LARGE COLLEGE

_____

_____

_____

_____

_____

_____

ADVANTAGES OF A SMALL COLLEGE

_____

_____

_____

_____

_____

_____

exercise 5

Look at your lists of advantages. In small groups, discuss whether large or small colleges are better for non-native English speaking students. Remember that some things may be more important than others.

exercise 6

Choose the topic you want to write about: the advantages of a large college or the advantages of a small college for immigrant or international students. Add to your list advantages other students mentioned that you think are important.

2. Organizing Ideas

Arranging Ideas in Order of Importance

> Now that you have some ideas about your topic, you need to organize them. One way of doing this is to write about the most important ideas first, then the less important ones.

Look at the lists of advantages you made in Exercises 4, 5, and 6. Which advantages are most important? Rank these advantages in order of importance, with number 1 as the most important. Cross out any advantages that are not very important.

Giving Reasons

> When you write, you should give reasons for your opinions.

On the lines below, list your advantages in order of importance. Then give at least one reason for each of the advantages. This will make an outline you can use when you write.

example: ADVANTAGE 1: Small schools have fewer students.
                REASON: It is easier to get to know the other students.

ADVANTAGE 1: _____

REASON: _____

ADVANTAGE 2: _____

REASON: _____

ADVANTAGE 3: _____

REASON: _____

ADVANTAGE 4: _____

REASON: _____

ADVANTAGE 5: _____

REASON: _____

ADVANTAGE 6: _____

REASON: _____

Writing Topic Sentences

> The topic sentence usually comes at the beginning of a paragraph. It tells the reader the main idea of the paragraph. A good topic sentence is neither too specific nor too general.

exercise **3**

Here is a list of possible topic sentences for a different paragraph about the advantages of studying abroad. Discuss them in groups or as a class. Are any topic sentences too specific or too general? There is no one correct answer.

1. Students who study abroad often can't speak the language well.
2. Studying abroad has three main advantages.
3. There are several reasons why students should study abroad.
4. There are many good schools in foreign countries.
5. If possible, all college students should spend some time studying in a foreign country.

An English class for international students

*exercise* **4**

Write a topic sentence for your paragraph about the advantages of large or small colleges. It can be similar to one of the topic sentences above.

_____

_____

*exercise* **5**

Have another student read your topic sentence and discuss how you might improve it. Read the other student's topic sentence. Answer the questions below.

1. Is it a complete sentence?
2. Does it tell the reader what you are going to write about?
3. Is it too general or too specific?

An international student and his advisor

3. Developing Cohesion and Style

Giving Reasons: *Because, So, Therefore*

When you give reasons for your ideas, you may want to use connectors that show cause or result.

Because appears in phrases and clauses that state a cause (a reason).

examples: *Because* large schools offer many different courses, students have a wide choice of subjects to take.
Students have a wide choice of subjects to take *because* large schools offer many different courses.

So and *therefore* appear in phrases and clauses that state a result.

examples: Large schools offer many different courses. *Therefore,* students have a wide choice of subjects to take.
Large schools offer many different courses, *so* students have a wide choice of subjects to take.

exercise 1   Complete the following sentences with *because, so,* or *therefore.* Note the different punctuation and capitalization in sentences with these three connectors.

1. Students who study in a foreign country live with people who do not speak their native language; _____, they will learn a foreign language well.

2. Public colleges in your own state are more practical _____ they are less expensive.

3. When students attend a local college, they can live at home _____ they don't have to spend a lot on rent and food.

4. _____ students have to study in a foreign language, they often have difficulty with their courses.

5. International students spend a long time away from home. _____, they may forget their own customs and culture.

Using Transition Words: *In addition, Also*

When you write a paragraph that lists information, you must use transition words—words that connect your ideas. If you don't use transition words, your paragraph will sound "choppy"—that is, not cohesive.

A writer can make a paragraph more cohesive by adding the transitions *also* and *in addition.*

examples: It is very difficult to study abroad. *In addition*, it can be much more expensive than studying in your own country. It is very difficult to study abroad. *Also*, it can be much more expensive than studying in your own country.

In addition usually comes at the beginning of a sentence. In this position, it always takes a comma.

Also can come at the beginning of a sentence, before a simple present or a past tense verb, or after an auxiliary verb or modal. If it comes at the beginning of a sentence, a comma always follows it.

exercise 2   Rewrite the paragraph below, using *also* and *in addition.*

WHY STUDY ABROAD?

Studying abroad offers students many advantages. The students live in a new culture, so they can learn both in and out of the classroom. They learn to be flexible because they have to adapt to different ways of living. They are far from home. Therefore, they have to become responsible and self-reliant. They have an experience they will remember all their lives.

 Use transition words *in addition* and *also* to connect these pairs of ideas.

   1. Undergraduate students are usually too immature to live away from home. They are too irresponsible.

   _____

   _____

   2. Most students in four-year colleges are very intelligent. They study hard.

   _____

   _____

   3. Professors in small colleges don't always understand international students. They may know very little about foreign cultures.

   _____

   _____

   4. Students who go abroad to study lose close contact with their families. Some of them marry foreigners and never return home.

   _____

   _____

Using Transition Words: *First of all, Finally*

Two other useful transitions are *first of all* and *finally*.

   examples: There are many reasons why international students feel homesick. *First of all*, it may be the first time they are away from their families . . . *Finally*, there is the problem of adapting to a completely different culture.

Note that *first of all* and *finally* always come at the beginning of a sentence and always take a comma.

exercise 4

Rewrite the paragraph below, using the transitions *in addition*, *also*, *first of all*, and *finally*. Remember to use commas where necessary.

There are several reasons that undergraduate students should not study away from home. Living away from home is much more expensive than living at home. Most teenagers are not mature enough to live far away from their families. Therefore, they often get into trouble. Many students feel lonely and homesick, so they are unable to study. Many who go away to study never return to their countries.

focus on testing

Editing for Transition Words

Exercises 2, 3, and 4 in this section gave you practice with transition words. Transition words make your writing smooth and easy to read, so when you write a paragraph for a timed test, make sure you've used transition words correctly. Save time *after* you write to reread your paragraph. Make sure that each sentence connects logically to the one before it with an appropriate transition word.

Moderating Opinions: Adverbs of Frequency and Quantifiers

When you state an opinion, you usually moderate it (make it less strong) with an adverb of frequency such as *sometimes, usually* or *often,* or a quantifier such as *some* or *many.* Also, be careful when you use a noun with no modifier. For example, in the sentence *International students work harder than American students,* it is important to add *many, most,* or *some* before the subject, *international students.*

exercise 5

Rewrite the following sentences, using adverbs of frequency and/or quantifiers.

1. All international students have a difficult time their first year.

_____

2. International students never become friendly with Americans.

_____

3. International students get better grades than American students.

_____

4. American professors don't understand international students.

_____

Other Adverbs of Frequency and Quantifiers

To moderate an opinion, you can also substitute other adverbs of frequency for _never_ or _always_ and other quantifiers for _all_ or _no._

1. Instead of _never_, use _rarely, almost never, hardly ever,_ or _usually . . . not._

    OPINION: Teachers never have time to discuss a student's personal problems.
    MODERATED: Teachers usually don't have time to discuss a student's personal problems.

2. Instead of _always_, use _usually, almost always,_ or _often._

    OPINION: First-year students always have roommate problems.
    MODERATED: First-year students often have roommate problems.

3. Instead of _all_, use _almost all, almost every, most,_ or _many._

    OPINION: All international students get homesick.
    MODERATED: Almost every international student gets homesick.

4. Instead of _no_ or _none_, use _very few, hardly any, almost no,_ or _almost none._

    OPINION: No international student learns English easily.
    MODERATED: Very few international students learn English easily.

Note: When you change _all_ to _almost every_ (in 3.) and _no_ to _very few_ (in 4.), the subject and verb forms change.

 **exercise 6** Substitute or add words and phrases to moderate these sentences.

1. Students in city colleges are too busy to be friendly.

_____

_____

2. Four-year colleges don't offer practical training.

_____

3. Studying in a foreign language is always very difficult.

_____

4. All students in community colleges can live at home.

_____

5. Studying in a private college is extremely expensive.

_____

4. Writing the First Draft

You have developed and organized your ideas and thought about the way you will write them. Now you are ready to write your paragraph. However, the paragraph you write will still need work; we call this paragraph a *draft*. A draft is an intermediate step, not the final product.

Write the first draft of your paragraph on the advantages of large or small colleges. Remember to include reasons for all of your opinions and to use transition words to connect your ideas. Write on every other line, so that it will be easy to make changes in your paragraph.

5. Editing Practice
Editing for Content and Form

You should edit paragraphs at least two times.

- The first time, look for problems in the content and organization of the paragraph.
- The second time, focus on the form of the paragraph: on the writer's grammar, punctuation, and spelling.

exercise 1 Edit the following paragraph for content. Focus only on the writer's ideas and organization. Use the questions below to help you edit. Make any content corrections you think are necessary.

- Does the writer give enough information?
- Does the writer give a reason for each opinion?
- Does the topic sentence give the main idea of the paragraph?
- Are the writer's arguments organized from most important to least important?
- Does the writer use transition words and connectors?
- Does the writer use adverbs of frequency and quantifiers?

There are several reasons that undergraduate students should not study away from home living away from home is much more expensive than living at home. Teenagerts are not mature enough to live far away from their families . Therefore, they often get into trou ble. Many students feel lonely and homesick

So they are not able to study.

Using Correct Paragraph Format

Here are some rules about the correct form of a paragraph. (For more rules on capitalization and punctuation, see Appendix Two and Appendix Three.)

1. Indent the first sentence of your paragraphs.
2. Leave a left and right margin.
3. Begin each sentence with a capital letter.
4. End each sentence with a period (.), a question mark (?), or an exclamation mark (!).
5. Make sure that the end punctuation immediately follows the last word of the sentence.
6. Leave a small space between sentences.
7. Divide words between syllables. (A dictionary will tell you where to divide a word if you aren't sure where the syllables begin and end.)
8. Never divide one-syllable words.

---

exercise 2 Now edit the paragraph a second time. This time, focus on the form. Use the rules in the box above to help you. Make any corrections you think are necessary. Then check your revised paragraph against the paragraph in Exercise 4 on page 10.

Making General Statements
with Present-Tense Verbs

In English, there are several ways to make statements that are generally true. Look at the sentences in the exercises in this unit and answer these questions:

1. What tense are the verbs?
2. Are the subjects usually singular or plural?
3. Does the article *the* usually precede the subjects?

You will notice that general statements are in the simple present tense and that the subjects are usually plural with no articles. When the subjects are people, singular personal pronouns can be awkward in English. For example, look at these sentences. Which sentence sounds awkward? Why?

> Students must leave their families.
> A student must leave his or her family.

When you are editing compositions that contain general statements, make sure that you follow these rules:

1. Use simple present verbs.
2. Add *-s* to verbs with third-person singular subjects (*he, she,* or *it*)
3. Count nouns should generally be plural with no article. (You will see more on the use of noncount nouns in Chapter Two.)
4. Pronouns must agree in number with their antecedents. *Every student should keep his or her culture* is correct although it is awkward. *Every student should keep their culture* would be wrong because *student* is singular.

exercise 3   The underlined words in the sentences below may be wrong. Edit the sentences according to the preceding four rules, changing the words that are incorrect. Some sentences may be correct.

1. Most family save for many years to send his children to college.
2. Students feel homesick.
3. Small schools don't have good library.
4. A large school has many students in their classes.
5. A school with many students aren't very friendly.
6. People who work can easily attend community colleges.

6. Editing Your Writing

Edit your first draft using the checklist below. First, check your paragraph for content, organization, cohesion and style using items 1, 2, and 3 in the checklist. Then edit your paragraph for grammar and form using items 4 and 5.

Editing Checklist

1. Content
   a. Did you include everything that you wanted to say?
   b. Did you give a reason for each opinion?
2. Organization
   a. Does your topic sentence give the main idea of your paragraph?
   b. Did you organize your ideas from most important to least important?
3. Cohesion and Style
   a. Did you use transition words and connectors?
   b. Did you use adverbs of frequency and quantifiers?
4. Grammar
   a. Did you use present tense verbs?
   b. Did you use adverbs of frequency and quantifiers?
5. Form
   a. Did you use correct paragraph format? (indentation, division of words between syllables, margins)
   b. Did you use correct punctuation? (capitalization, commas, periods)
   c. Did you check the spelling of words you were not sure of?

Show your paragraph to another student. She or he will check your work and tell you if anything is unclear.

7. Writing the Second Draft

After you edit your paragraph, rewrite it neatly, using good handwriting and correct form. Give your second draft to your teacher for comments. When your teacher returns your paper, ask him or her about any comments or corrections you don't understand. The next time you write, look back at your teacher's comments. Follow your teacher's instructions and try not to make the same mistakes again.

A STEP beyond

activity 1

Use the paragraphs the class wrote for this chapter for a debate.

1. Divide into two groups: students who think that small colleges are better for international students and students who prefer large colleges.
2. Meet with members of your team and read one another's compositions.
3. Make a list of your arguments.
4. Try to guess what the other team will argue and think of reasons against their arguments. (These are called *rebuttals*.)
5. Choose three students to represent each side. One gives the arguments (about five minutes), one the rebuttal (about three minutes), and one the summary (about three minutes).

activity 2

Write another paragraph about the advantages or disadvantages of one of the following topics (or choose your own topic).

1. small towns / large cities
2. bilingual education / monolingual education
3. city colleges / colleges in the country
4. small families / large families
5. an arts degree / a science degree
6. life today / life in the past

activity 3

Look through some magazines and read the advertisements for different products. Choose an ad that shows a product's advantages. Make a list of all the advantages it describes. Give your list and the picture without the text to a partner. See if he or she can write the text using your list. Then compare your partner's ad with the real ad. How are they different? How are they the same?

Journal Writing

Start to keep a journal. In this journal, write whatever ideas come into your head. Your teacher may ask you to write in your journal in class or at home. Don't worry about grammar or correct form. Concentrate on expressing your ideas.

activity 4

Choose one of the following topics.

1. Start now and write for ten minutes about anything you want. If you can't think of anything to say, write about how you can't think of anything.
2. Write in your journal about your school and/or your English class. What do you like about it? What do you dislike? What do you find difficult? What is easy for you?

CHAPTER **two**

City Life

You will write a description of the place where you live.

in this chapter

STEPS TO **writing**

1. Exploring Ideas
Describing Scenes

exercise 1 Look at these pictures of city streets and choose one of them to describe. Write as much as you can in ten minutes. You can answer some of these questions.

1. What kind of street is this?
2. What is happening on the street?
3. What kinds of people live on this street?
4. How do you feel about the street?
5. How is the street similar to or different from the street where you live?

exercise 2 In small groups, discuss what you wrote with a few other students who wrote about the same picture. Did you notice the same things in the picture? Did you feel the same way about the street?

Including Sense Details and Feelings

> You are going to write a personal description of the place where you live: your neighborhood, your street, your dorm, your apartment or house, or your room. A good description includes *sense details:* the things you can see, hear, touch, taste, and smell.

 **exercise 3**   Write the name of the place you are going to describe here (for instance, "My Neighborhood"):

_____

WHAT DO YOU THINK?

Classifying Sense Details

Sense details make a description come alive. Work with a partner and test your knowledge of words used to describe things you see, hear, smell, taste, and touch. Classify the following adjectives by putting them in the correct category. (Note: Some might fit into more than one category.) Add some of your own.

noisy	salty	sour	dry	sticky	rotten
bitter	colorful	bright	sweet	dark	tight
rough	gloomy	foul	delicate		

SEE	HEAR	SMELL	TASTE	TOUCH
___	___	___	___	___
___	___	___	___	___
___	___	___	___	___
___	___	___	___	___
___	___	___	___	___

Now give an example of each word to show you know what it means.

 **exercise 4**   Now make a list of sense details for the place you are going to describe.

1. What I can see:

_____

_____

2. What I can hear:

_____

_____

3. What I can touch:

_____

_____

4. What I can taste (optional):

_____

_____

5. What I can smell (optional):

_____

_____

exercise 5   A personal description also includes the feelings and opinions the writer has about the place he or she is describing. Write a few notes about *how* you feel about the place you describe. Also write about *why* you feel the way you do.

_____

_____

_____

_____

 **exercise 6**   Describe the place you chose to a partner. Ask each other questions about the places you describe.

Building Vocabulary

> If you use specific descriptive words, you can make your paragraph more interesting.

   Read the following paragraph. The descriptive words and phrases are underlined. Discuss the meanings of unfamiliar items and tell which sense they describe.

MY NEIGHBORHOOD

Since people from all over the world live in my neighborhood, it is a fascinating place to explore. When I walk down the main street of the neighborhood, I can hear the babble of languages from all over the globe. Each language is accompanied by a colorful ethnic shop or exotic restaurant. On a warm evening, I can smell the sweet melons from the Korean produce store or the aroma of freshly baked bread from the Hungarian bakery. These smells are free, but for a small price I can also buy any of fifty kinds of cheeses with unpronounceable names from one store or strange Asian vegetables and the spices to liven them up from another. The people of the neighborhood take pride in their surroundings. They build neighborhood churches, synagogues, and clubs in all different architectural styles. On almost every street, they plant trees and flowers from their native countries to remind them of home and to brighten up the dreary gray cement and run-down apartment buildings. One neighbor of mine plants delicate Scottish flowers every year in memory of her mother's garden in Scotland. Another neighbor has a Chinese vegetable garden in window boxes. I don't need to buy an airplane ticket to experience the world; a walk around my neighborhood can be just as exciting.

Choose one of these pictures. In small groups, make lists of words that describe the neighborhood. Then use those words to describe the picture.

1. What you can see:

_____

2. What you can hear:

_____

3. What you can smell:

_____

4. What you can taste:

_____

5. What you can feel:

_____

2. Organizing Ideas
Writing Topic Sentences

The topic sentence gives the main idea of a paragraph. It is often the first sentence in the paragraph and should express an idea you can easily write about in one paragraph. The topic sentence should not be too general. If it is, there will be too much to write about, and you will need more than one paragraph.

Also, a good topic sentence should have a clear _focus._ This means it should present a _particular_ idea, feeling, or opinion about the topic.

Too general: My neighborhood is a nice place to live.
A good topic sentence: My neighborhood is fascinating because people from many countries live in it.

 **_exercise_ 1**

In each pair of topic sentences below, identify the one sentence that is too general and the one that has a clear focus.

1. Topic: "My Room"
  a. My room is a perfect place for one person to live.
  b. Many people live in single rooms.

2. Topic: "My House"
  a. There are a lot of houses like mine in my neighborhood.
  b. I love my house because it is filled with happy memories.

3. Topic: "My Dormitory"
  a. My dormitory has never felt like home to me.
  b. I live in a dormitory.

 **_exercise_ 2**

Write a topic sentence for your own paragraph. Then in small groups, discuss each others' topic sentences. Are any of them too general? Do they express a particular feeling or an opinion about the topic?

_____

_____

Adding Details to a Paragraph

The other sentences in the paragraph should develop the idea in the topic sentence. Look at the details that the writer is going to use to develop this topic sentence.

Topic sentence: My neighborhood is fascinating because people from many countries live in it.

- great shops—German butcher shop, Hungarian bakery, Korean produce store, French cheese store
- the food from the shops smells good
- ethnic restaurants
- many different languages
- woman next door plants flowers to remind her of Scotland
- beautiful churches and synagogues

A Ukrainian shop in New York City

exercise **3**

Make notes you could use for sentences to develop your topic sentence. These notes are just ideas for you to think about. You don't have to use all the notes you make, and when you are writing your paragraph you may think of other ideas to write about.

_____

_____

_____

_____

_____

Checking That All the Details Develop the Topic Sentence

> All the details in the paragraph should develop the idea given in the topic sentence.

 **exercise 4**   In the following list, one detail is not on the topic. Find it and cross it out.

> *Topic sentence:* My room is small, but it is very cozy and has everything I need.

- is small but has enough space for my things, with a big closet
- has a big window with a view of a beautiful oak tree where there are often birds and squirrels
- landlord is not very pleasant
- is on the second floor and is quiet
- is nice and warm in winter
- has a small refrigerator and a cabinet for dishes

 **exercise 5**   Look at the details you wrote for your paragraph and show them to a partner. Add any others you can think of and cross out the ones that are not on the topic.

focus on testing

Brainstorming for Ideas

In this section, you practiced writing topic sentences and adding details to a paragraph. When you're in a test-taking situation, you have little time to do these things. So take some time *before* you write to brainstorm. First, list all the ideas that come to your mind about the topic. Then read your list and see what main idea it suggests. (Cross out any ideas that don't fit.) Use your main idea to write a topic sentence. Use the rest of your ideas to develop your paragraph: group the ones that go together, and number them in the order you want to write about them.

Writing Concluding Sentences

Most paragraphs have concluding sentences, which may repeat the idea of the topic sentence in different words or give a personal reaction to the topic of the paragraph. Here is a concluding sentence for the ideas about the ethnic neighborhood in the box on page 24.

I don't need to buy an airplane ticket to experience the world; a walk around my neighborhood is just as exciting.

Here is a good concluding sentence for a paragraph about how a Brazilian student felt about living in a dorm with no other students from Brazil.

Although I often felt lonely and homesick at first, I feel that I made some good American friends because I didn't have people from Brazil to talk with.

 **exercise 6**   Give examples of some possible concluding sentences for these topics.

1. living in an apartment with two sloppy roommates

_____

_____

2. living in a run-down neighborhood where there's a lot of crime

_____

_____

3. living with your family

_____

_____

4. living in an old house

_____

_____

5. living in a small room in a modern dorm

_____

_____

3. Developing Cohesion and Style

Giving Reasons: *Since*

Because and *since* have almost the same meaning. *Because* and *since* often appear in dependent clauses in complex sentences. Look at the following examples of complex sentences with *since*. The dependent clauses are underlined.

> examples: Since quite a few people in the neighborhood come from Germany, there are many great German shops and restaurants here.
>
> There are many great German shops and restaurants here since quite a few people in the neighborhood come from Germany.

Note that a dependent clause with *since* can come at the beginning or the end of the sentence. If a clause with *since* begins a sentence, you usually use a comma after it. You don't use a comma if the clause comes at the end of the sentence.

exercise  Combine these sentences using *since*. Remember to use a comma after the clause if you put it at the beginning of the sentence.

1. Many people have lived in my neighborhood for years. It is a very friendly place.

   _____

   _____

2. My apartment is small. I have to keep it very neat.

   _____

   _____

3. My street is often dirty and smells like garbage. Many food stores are on it.

   _____

   _____

4. It is easy to get to know everyone in my dorm. Only forty people live in it.

   _____

   _____

Varying Word Order in Sentences

If most of the sentences in a paragraph begin the same way, the paragraph may be boring to read. For example:

My neighborhood is a wonderful place to eat and shop for food because people from all over the world live there. My neighborhood has a lot of different ethnic restaurants since the people come from many countries. My neighborhood is the best place to go when you want some good Chinese, Italian, Ukrainian, Vietnamese, or Polish food. My neighborhood is also the greatest when you want to buy many kinds of international foods. You can buy delicious cheeses and sausages at the Italian store on the corner of my block. You can buy sweet melons and all kinds fresh vegetables from the Korean produce store two blocks from my apartment. You can also buy freshly baked bread and pastries in the Hungarian bakery across the street. Why would I want to live anywhere else when everything I need is right in my neighborhood?

You can make the paragraph more interesting for a reader if you vary the word order in some of the sentences. For example, you can begin some of the sentences with dependent clauses (beginning with words like *because, since,* and *when*) or prepositional phrases (beginning with words such as *at, in, on, from, with*).

 Look back at the paragraph in Exercise 7 on page 21. Which sentences in the paragraph begin with dependent clauses or prepositional phrases? Note that a comma generally comes after a beginning clause or phrase.

 Rewrite the example paragraph from the box above. Vary the word order in some of the sentences to make the paragraph more interesting to read. When you finish, compare your paragraph with that of another classmate. Are your revised paragraphs similar?

4. Writing the First Draft

Write your paragraph using the topic sentence you wrote and the notes you made. Make your paragraph interesting by adding details and varying word order in your sentences. Don't worry about grammar when you write the first draft. Write on every other line so you can revise your paragraph.

International products are available at this grocery store in New York City.

5. Editing Practice

Correcting Run-On Sentences

A run-on sentence is an incorrect sentence made of two independent sentences connected with a comma.

> *Run-on:* I am living in a dorm room, it is much too small for my roommate and me.
> *Run-on:* First you notice all the exciting sights, later you notice the dirt.

You can correct a run-on sentence in at least three ways.

1. Change the comma to a period or a semicolon.

   I am living in a dorm room. It is much too small for my roommate and me.
   First you notice all the exciting sights; later you notice the dirt.

2. Change the run-on sentence into a sentence with a dependent clause. The dependent clause is underlined in the example.

   I am living in a dorm room <u>that is much too small for my roommate and me</u>.

   In this example, the dependent clause is an adjective clause that modifies (describes) the noun *dorm room.* The pronoun *that* replaces *it* and is the subject of the adjective clause.

3. Use a conjunction such as *and, but,* or *so* to connect the two independent sentences. Note that a comma usually comes before the conjunction.

First you notice all the exciting sights, *and* later you notice the dirt.

The following words often begin new sentences, but students sometimes use them after commas in run-on sentences. Check for them when you edit.

it   he   she   they   then   however   therefore   later

Correct these run-on sentences.

1. My suburban apartment is big and sunny, it has a living room with large windows filled with plants.
2. I have a roommate who is very sloppy, she never washes the dishes, and she leaves her clothes all over the apartment.
3. I like my street because my neighbors are wonderful, they will help anybody who is having problems.
4. I fixed up my room this fall. First I painted it a pale blue, later I made new curtains.
5. My favorite place to relax is the park, it is up the hill from my apartment.
6. My street is dirty and noisy, however it has many good restaurants and everyone on it is friendly.

Edit this paragraph for run-on sentences and rewrite it correctly.

My neighborhood is a fascinating place, it is in one of the biggest cities in the world, New York City, however, there is a small-town feeling to it. Most of the buildings in the neighborhood are small brick apartment houses, they have peeling red and brown paint. Many of the people here have lived in the neighborhood for years, they know each other and take pride in the neighborhood. They have planted trees and flowers in front of the buildings, they have built benches where the old people sit and talk. Since many of the people are from Germany and Eastern Europe, there are wonderful German, Hungarian, and Polish shops here. I wouldn't want to live in any other neighborhood of the city.

Editing with the Topic Sentence in Mind

All of the sentences in a paragraph should develop the main idea in the topic sentence. If they don't, there are two things you can do:

1. Maybe you started to write about an idea that is different from the idea in your topic sentence. If you like the idea, you should change your topic sentence.
2. Maybe some of your sentences are not about the idea in your topic sentence. You should cross out those sentences.

exercise **3** Look at the following paragraph. Should the writer change the topic sentence or cross out some sentences? Correct the paragraph according to your decision about each. There may be several correct ways to revise the paragraph.

I live in an ordinary house on an ordinary street in an ordinary suburb, and I think it is terrific! My house is now about thirty years old, but it looks newer. I used to live in a small apartment, first in Florida, and then in New Mexico. It is like hundreds of other houses in the suburbs, one story with an attached garage. There is nothing special about the house, and it won't win any prizes for architecture, but it's perfect for my family. The kitchen is big and has new appliances, including a washing machine and dryer. I hate the heat, but we have air conditioning in the living room and bedrooms, so it is always cool. I don't know why some Americans I know don't like the suburbs. For the kids there's a nice yard where they can play. I am very thankful that we can afford this house and live our ordinary lives in it.

Using Noncount Nouns

Many nouns in English are always singular because they are *noncount*—you can't count them. Which of these nouns are noncount?

bakery	cement	pride	village
bread	neighborhood	lettuce	world

Nouns that are countable in some languages may be noncount nouns in English. Check the chart in the appendix in the back of the book for a list of common noncount nouns. When you edit your paragraph, check it to see if you have used noncount nouns correctly.

6. Editing Your Writing

 *exercise 1*

Edit your first draft using the checklist below. First, check your paragraph for content, organization, cohesion and style using items 1, 2, and 3 in the checklist. Then edit your paragraph for grammar and form using items 4 and 5.

Editing Checklist

1. Content
    a. Did you add enough descriptive details?
    b. Did you use a variety of adjectives?
2. Organization
    a. Is your topic sentence the main idea of your paragraph?
    b. Do all the details develop the topic sentence?
    c. Did you include a concluding sentence?
3. Cohesion and Style
    a. Have you given reasons for your feelings?
    b. Have you varied the word order of your sentences?
4. Grammar
    a. Did you avoid run-on sentences?
    b. Did you use correct verb forms?
5. Form
    a. Did you use correct paragraph format? (indentation, division of words between syllables, margins)
    b. Did you use correct punctuation? (capitalization, commas, periods)
    c. Did you check the spelling of words you were not sure of?

Exchange paragraphs with another student. Does she or he understand your paragraph? Does she or he think you need to make any corrections?

7. Writing the Second Draft

After you edit your paragraph, rewrite it neatly, using good handwriting and correct form. Give your second draft to your teacher for comments.

 **beyond**

Work in small groups. Take turns reading your paragraphs without their topic sentences. Your classmates will suggest some good topic sentences. Did anyone suggest a sentence that was similar to yours?

Look at the paragraphs in a description of your school (from a brochure or a school catalog) or in a selection you use for reading. Try to find the topic sentence of each paragraph. Did some topic sentences come in the middle or the end of the paragraph? How many paragraphs had no topic sentences?

Find other descriptions of people, places, or things. Which descriptions are personal (including feelings and opinions)? Which descriptions are impersonal (including facts, not feelings)? Did the writer use sense details? If so, how?

Write a brief description of a common object—for example, a pencil, a brick wall, or a telephone. Don't write the name of the object, but include as many details as possible in the description. In small groups, take turns reading your descriptions. Can your classmates guess what you are describing?

Journal Writing

Write in your journal about one or both of the following topics.

1. Write two descriptions of a person you know. Write each description in ten minutes. Make the first impersonal, including only facts. Make the second personal, including feelings and opinions.
2. Chose a topic you would like your partner to write about in his or her journal. Write about the topic your partner chooses for you.

CHAPTER three

Business and Money

in this chapter

You are going to write a letter to the editor in response to a newspaper article about people who took money that didn't belong to them.

STEPS TO **WRITING**

1. Exploring Ideas
Discussing Attitudes Toward Money

exercise 1

Read these famous quotations and proverbs about money. In small groups, discuss the sayings. Do you agree with them or not? What attitude toward money does each one express?

> If possible, make money honestly; if not, make it by any means. —*Horace (65–8 B.C.)*

If you would know the value of money, go and try to borrow some; for he that goes a-borrowing goes sorrowing. Time is money. —*Benjamin Franklin (1706–1790)*

Money is indeed the most important thing in the world; and all sound and successful personal and national morality should have this fact for its basis. —*George Bernard Shaw (1856–1950)*

Money speaks sense in a language all nations understand. —*Aphra Behn (1640–1689)*

And money is like muck, not good except it be spread. —*Francis Bacon (1561–1626)*

Money is our madness, our vast collective madness. —*D. H. Lawrence (1885–1930)*

It has been said that the love of money is the root of all evil. —*Samuel Butler (1835–1902)*

Money buys everything except love, personality, freedom, immortality, silence, peace. —*Carl Sandburg (1878–1967)*

 **exercise 2** Translate a quotation or a proverb about money from your own language into English. Discuss the quotations with a partner. What attitudes toward money do they show?

 **exercise 3** Write as much as you can in ten minutes about your own attitude toward money.

 **exercise 4** In small groups, read the newspaper article below and discuss the different people's reactions to the event it describes. You are going to write a letter to the editor in response to it.

Luck or Thievery?

COLUMBUS, OHIO. October 28 was a lucky day for motorists driving along Interstate 71 at about 9:30 in the morning. As a truck from the Metropolitan Armored Car Company sped down the highway, its back door blew open, spilling bags of money onto the road. When other vehicles hit the bags, they split open, spewing out a million dollars.

It didn't take motorists long to realize that the paper swirling around them was hard cash. They stopped on and around the highway and scooped up handfuls of money, gleefully cramming $20, $50, $100, even $1,000 dollar bills into bags, pockets, and purses. When the police arrived, they estimated that two hundred people were helping themselves to this bonanza.

Officials hoping to recover this money were not so gleeful. Columbus Mayor Dana

G. Rinehart called these people thieves and said, "May they have many sleepless nights." He claims the government will prosecute anyone the police can find.

To encourage the return of the money, Metropolitan Armored Car has offered a reward of 10% of all the money they receive. So far, however, they have received only $100,000—from about thirty different people. One man turned in $57,000. Another man, however, called to say he was set for life and was leaving town. Since the cash was insured and belonged to local banks, many people can't see that they are hurting real people by keeping it.

Even if the government prosecutes, it will have trouble convicting the thieves. "Probably two-thirds of the jurors would think the defendant should have kept the money," said prosecutor Michael Miller.

Building Vocabulary

You can guess the meanings of many of the new words in the newspaper article from context. Match these vocabulary words with their meanings.

1. _____ armored
2. _____ split
3. _____ spew
4. _____ swirl
5. _____ scoop up
6. _____ gleeful
7. _____ bonanza
8. _____ prosecute
9. _____ convict

a. very happy
b. pick up
c. charge with a crime
d. tear open
e. move in circles
f. spill
g. something of great value
h. protected with strong metal
i. find guilty of a crime

In your response, you might want to use some of the words that you weren't familiar with. First categorize them into parts of speech. Then make sentences with six of the words, giving your opinion of the happenings in the article.

NOUNS	VERBS	ADJECTIVES
		armored

example: Maybe the drivers of the *armored* car didn't lock the doors intentionally.

2. Organizing Ideas
Writing Reactions to a Reading Selection

Discuss these questions in small groups.

1. Is it wrong to keep money that you haven't earned?
2. What does it mean that the money is *insured*? Who will pay back the money? Is it true that the loss of the money doesn't hurt anyone?
3. What would you do if you were one of the motorists? Would you take the money? What would you do if you were an official of the town?

exercise 2   Should the motorists return the money? Write reasons why or why not below.

REASONS WHY THE MOTORISTS SHOULD RETURN THE MONEY

_____

_____

_____

_____

_____

_____

REASONS WHY THE MOTORISTS SHOULD NOT RETURN THE MONEY

_____

_____

_____

_____

_____

_____

_____

exercise 3   Read what you wrote about your attitude toward money in Exercise 3 on page 37. Do you think the motorists should or should not return the money? Does your attitude toward money support your opinion?

Analyzing the Organization of a Letter to the Editor

Read this letter to the editor of a newspaper.

Home Free

Regarding the report on Americans who don't pay taxes on money they make from small home businesses (Oct. 23): My opinion is that the government should stay out of at least one part of our lives.

First of all, most people who run these small businesses are law-abiding citizens. Many of them have other jobs where they pay more than their share of taxes (unlike the wealthy, who pay almost none). Others are people who want jobs where they have to pay taxes, but can't find them.

Secondly, the government requires too much paperwork from small businesses.

If these small businesspeople have to keep the complicated records that the tax people require, they won't have time to sell old furniture, prepare food for parties, or whatever their business involves.

Finally, and most importantly, the United States is supposed to be a free country, but the government interferes everywhere. Let us Americans be free at least in our own homes!

Al Melinowski

Ann Walker prepares tax returns from her home office.

Mike Brukowski caters parties from his home kitchen.

exercise 4 Answer these questions about the letter.

1. How does the letter begin and end?
2. How many paragraphs does the letter have? Are the paragraphs long or short? (Note that paragraphs in newspapers are often shorter than paragraphs in academic writing.)
3. What transition expressions does the writer use?
4. How does the writer support his opinions?

exercise 5 Write an opening sentence for your letter responding to "Luck or Thievery" similar to the opening sentence of "Home Free." Begin with a phrase telling which article you are responding to: *"Regarding . . ."* or *"In response to . . ."* Give the name and date of the article and then tell your opinion.

exercise 6 Now give two or three reasons for your opinion:

_____

_____

_____

3. Developing Cohesion and Style

Stating Obligations and Opinions with Modals: *Must, Have to, Should, Ought to*

> You can show the strength of your opinion by the choice of the modal you use.

exercise 1 Which of the modals *must, have to, should,* and *ought to* show strong obligation or duty? Which show weaker obligation? Find an example of *should* and an example of *have to* in the letter to the editor on page 40. Why do you think the writer used those modals in those instances?

exercise 2 Make sentences using *must, must not, have to, not have to, should, should not,* or *ought to* about the following topics, depending on how strong you think the obligation is.

> **example:** Every working person *should* pay taxes, but many people don't.

1. paying taxes
2. drinking alcohol
3. drinking alcohol and then driving

4. spending a lot of money to clean up the environment
5. giving money to the poor
6. gambling
7. trying to find the owner of some jewelry you found on the street
8. robbing a person's house if you need money
9. borrowing someone's car

Supporting an Opinion with a General Statement and Examples

 Look at the second paragraph in the letter to the editor on page 40. It gives a general truth and then supports it with examples. What is the general truth? What are the examples?

*General truth:*_____

*Examples:*_____

_____

 These sentences state general truths. Give one or two examples to support them.

1. The government loses millions of dollars every year because of people who don't pay their share of taxes.

_____

_____

2. Almost everyone gambles in one way or another.

_____

_____

3. Money is the root of all evil.

_____

_____

4. Lack of money is the root of much of the evil of our society.

_____

_____

5. When you find something on the street that someone has lost, it is almost impossible to find the owner.

_____

_____

 Look at the reasons you gave in Exercise 2 on page 39 for your opinion on the newspaper article. Can you support any of them with examples?

Supporting an Opinion with Predictions

 Look at the third paragraph in the letter to the editor on page 40. It supports a general statement with a prediction. What is the prediction?

_____

What verb tense is used in the *if* clause?

_____

What verb tense is used in the main clause?

_____

 In small groups, make predictions. What will happen if . . .

1. the government opens (or closes) gambling casinos in your city?
2. the government starts (or prohibits) a lottery in your city?
3. the government makes the wealthy pay more taxes?
4. the government cuts welfare payments?
5. everyone gives one-tenth of his or her income to charity?
6. fewer drunk drivers are on the road?
7. the government makes smoking completely illegal in your town?
8. someone tries to return a valuable item he or she found on the street?

 Look at the reasons you gave for your opinion on the newspaper article. Can you support any of them with predictions?

focus on testing

Supporting Your Opinion

In this section, you've seen two ways to support an opinion. If you know you are going to take a timed test that requires you to give your opinion, it's a good idea to come to the test prepared to support it. To do this, think of topics you have covered in class or read news magazines to find current topics of interest *before* the test. Practice stating your opinion and supporting it with predictions or examples. This way, you'll be more comfortable with thinking of supporting reasons under time pressure.

Stating Opinions: Strong and Moderate

Some letters to the editor express opinions strongly and others do so moderately. A strong opinion does not usually allow for different points of view, whereas a moderate opinion does. When writers express their opinions strongly, they often use more emotional arguments. When writers express their opinions moderately, they often use more logical arguments.

exercise 9 Read the following expressions. Which of them are strong? Which are more moderate? How can you tell?

	STRONG	MODERATE
1. I disagree with . . .	_____	_____
2. . . . is total nonsense.	_____	_____
3. My opinion is that . . .	_____	_____
4. . . . is immoral.	_____	_____
5. . . . is the most logical solution.	_____	_____
6. Only a fool would disagree with . . .	_____	_____
7. I believe . . .	_____	_____
8. In my opinion . . .	_____	_____
9. . . . is completely absurd.	_____	_____

exercise 10 Create some sentences about the newspaper article using the preceding expressions. Which do you think are more appropriate for your letter?

_____

_____

_____

_____

_____

_____

_____

_____

_____

_____

4. Writing the First Draft

Write your letter using the opening sentence you wrote. Give your opinions and the reasons for your opinions, supporting them with examples or predictions. Don't worry about grammar at this time. Write on every other line so you can revise your paragraph. Add transitions to your paragraph.

5. Editing Practice
Avoiding Faulty Reasoning

When you revise a piece of writing that gives reasons for opinions, you should make sure that you haven't used *faulty reasoning*. Following are definitions and examples of different kinds of faulty reasoning.

1. False analogy: comparing two things that are not similar

   example: Some people have to gamble. They are just like thieves because they can hurt other people.

2. Generalization: saying that something is true for all when it is only true for some, or making a general statement based on only a few cases

   examples: All Americans are rich.
   There is a wealthy man who comes into the restaurant where I am a waiter and never leaves a tip. Rich men are stingy.
   (Note that in this example the generalization follows the description of one particular case.)

3. Irrelevant argument: giving an example or reason that does not relate to the opinion

   example: I don't think the accountant was embezzling money from his company because he has a nice family and always goes to church.

An irrelevant argument might also suggest that because one thing follows another, it relates to it, when it really doesn't.

example: Borrowing money always causes problems. Two days after Mario borrowed money, his wife asked for a divorce.

4. Begging the question: giving a reason that only restates the opinion in different words

example: Gambling is wrong because it is immoral.

exercise 1 The following statements are responses to the newspaper article you read, "Luck or Thievery." Identify the kind of faulty reasoning each one shows.

1. Everyone should return the money because the money should go back to the government.
2. I heard about a woman who got some of the money and didn't return it. The next day she fell and broke her leg. She knew she did the wrong thing.
3. Insurance companies always cheat people.
4. Picking up the money that fell onto the road is similar to picking flowers that grow in the forest.

exercise 2 Look at the reasons and examples you wrote in your letter. Do any of them show faulty reasoning?

WHAT DO YOU THINK?

Evaluating Arguments for Faulty Reasoning

Evaluating an argument for faulty reasoning is an important critical thinking skill. Practice this skill by listening to a talk show program on the radio or TV, or reading a letter to the editor in a supermarket *tabloid*. (A *tabloid* is a small newspaper with many pictures. Tabloids usually focus on strange or sensational news. They are often not carefully edited for faulty reasoning.) Take notes on the person's opinion and the reasons given for her or his opinion. Discuss your notes in small groups, telling group members the opinion and the reasons given. Discuss whether or not the person used faulty reasoning.

Correcting Spelling Errors

Always edit your writing for spelling errors. This is a good time to review the spelling rules in Appendix One. However, you can't always count on rules to help you with spelling. Often you have to use a dictionary to check words you are not sure you have spelled correctly.

 Correct these words if they are incorrect or write *correct* if they are correct. Use your dictionary if you are not sure.

1. successful _____

2. moralety _____

3. evil _____

4. honnestly _____

5. truely _____

6. estimatted _____

7. defendant _____

8. prosecutor _____

9. government _____

10. taxs _____

Correcting Syllabification Errors

If a word is too long to fit at the end of the line, divide it between syllables and put the second part of the word on the next line. Don't divide words that have one syllable. Put at least three letters on each line, and use a hyphen after the first part of the divided word. Look at these examples:

Incorrect: We couldn't find the place they told us about.

Correct: We couldn't find the
place they told us about.

Incorrect: He's always borrowing money.

Correct: He's always borrowing money.

or:
He's always bor-
rowing money.

General Rules for Syllabification

1. Divide words after prefixes or before suffixes.

   con-struc-tion   em-bez-zle-ment   com-fort-a-ble

2. Divide words between two consonants.

   col-lege   ad-dic-tion   com-pul-sive

   If you are not sure how to divide a word, write the whole word on the next line or check your dictionary.

If these words didn't fit at the end of a line, how would you divide them? Draw a line between syllables. Check your dictionary if necessary.

1. expensive   3. irrelevant   5. consumer   7. argument
2. accounting   4. organization   6. generous   8. immoral

Edit this paragraph. Find seventeen spelling errors, four syllabification errors, and three run-on sentences.

A PROBLEM WITH PRIORITIES

Pacific College spends too much money on activitys that are not related to educattion. One of the bigest expenses is athletics, for example, it has to pay for coaches' saliries, equipment, and building stadiems. It also sponsors a free student newspaper and many student activaties such as partys, plays, and conserts. Many staf members spend a lot of time organizing and planing these activities, they have to be paid salaries for this work as well. These activatys are fine, but not when the college is decresing libery hours on the weekends and increasing class size I like football games, partys, and conserts, but I beleive that my educattion is more important.

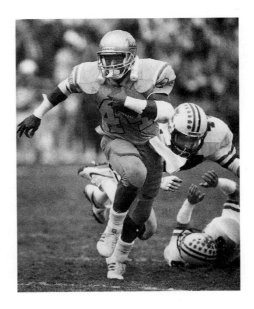

6. Editing Your Writing

 Edit your letter using the checklist below. First, check your paragraph for content, organization, cohesion, and style using items 1, 2, and 3 in the checklist. Then edit your paragraph for grammar and form using items 4 and 5.

Editing Checklist

1. Content
   a. Did you state your opinion clearly?
   b. Did you support your opinion with reasons?
   c. Did you support your reasons with examples and/or predictions?
   d. Did you avoid faulty reasoning?
2. Organization
   a. Did you write an opening sentence that told what article you were responding to and that gave your opinion?
   b. Did you write a concluding sentence?
3. Cohesion and style
   a. Did you use transitions?
   b. Did you state your opinions using appropriate modals?
   c. Did you use a moderate or a strong style to express your opinions?
4. Grammar
   a. Did you use simple verb forms with modals?
   b. Did you use present verb forms in *if* clauses and future verb forms in predictions?
   c. Did you avoid run-on sentences?
5. Form
   a. Did you use correct paragraph format: indentation, margins, capitals at beginning of sentences?
   b. Did you use correct spelling and syllabification?

 Exchange papers with another classmate and edit each other's paragraphs. Circle or underline in pencil any words, phrases, or sentences that you don't understand or that you think need to be corrected. Then return your paragraphs. Discuss any questions you have with your partner.

7. Writing the Second Draft

After you edit your letter, rewrite it neatly, using good handwriting and correct form. Sign your name and write your city at the bottom.

A STEP beyond

activity 1　Tape your letters to the board in two groups: one group for letters saying that the people should give the money back, and another group for the letters saying that the people shouldn't. Go to the board and read some of the letters. What reasons were given for each opinion? Are you and your classmates in general agreement or are there many differing opinions?

activity 2

Read some letters with opinions opposite to yours. Make a list of reasons why their arguments are not logical or true. Then get into teams and have a debate on the topic. (Students not on the debate teams can be the audience.) Students on both teams take turns presenting the reasons for their opinions; then both teams give their counterarguments. Finally, each team sums up. The audience can vote on which side won the debate.

activity 3　Look at a local, international, or school newspaper or magazine and find the letters to the editor. Often some are logical and others are emotional; some are serious and others try to be funny. Which letters do you like? Do they give strong or moderate opinions?

activity 4　Find an article or letter in a newspaper and write a letter in response to it.

activity 5　Have you experienced or heard about a strange happening like the one described in the newspaper article in this chapter? Write a description of the happening. Share your description with another classmate.

Journal Writing

activity 6　Write in your journal about one or more of these topics.

1. Write a letter to your teacher telling him or her what you like about the writing course and what you have learned. Then write about a suggestion you have for improving the course. You can give this to your teacher if you like.
2. Write your reaction to one of the proverbs or sayings at the beginning of this chapter or to one a classmate has told.
3. Write the word "BUSINESS" in the center of a page. Then quickly, without thinking, write around it any words, phrases or ideas you associate with the word. Use some of these words or ideas to write about your opinion of business.
4. Ask a classmate if you can read a selection from his or her journal. Write your reaction to the selection.

CHAPTER four

Jobs and Professions

in this chapter

You are going to write a reply to this job or college application instruction: *Describe an accomplishment in your life.*

STEPS TO **writing**

1. Exploring Ideas
Discussing Accomplishments

On application forms (and during personal interviews), many North American colleges and employers ask applicants questions about their past experience. These questions may require applicants to describe some personal accomplishments. In discussing a question about personal accomplishments, you want to show that you are special or different in some way. You should be positive and focus on your good points. Give enough information to show how you are special, but not too much: You don't want to seem like you are exaggerating or bragging.

 **exercise 1**   Look at the instructions from parts of various college and job applications on page 53. As a class or in small groups, discuss the reactions of the students in the pictures to the question *"What have you accomplished in the past two years?"* What do you think about their reactions? Do you feel similarly about this question?

 **exercise 2**   Discuss with your teacher the cultural attitudes toward describing accomplishments in your country and North America. Do employers and colleges expect you to focus on your successes or do they expect you to be humble and not write much about your successes? If you are applying to a North American company or college, how should you describe your past experiences? What should you avoid discussing (for example, religion, which is a private matter in North America)?

I hate filling out these applications! I never know what to say about myself!

But you've accomplished a lot during the last two years. You immigrated to the States, you're learning English, and you had a baby!

What have you accomplished in the past two years?

Tell us something about yourself that will help us know you better.

Write a short personal history.

Write about the most difficult thing you have ever done.

Discuss your duties in your previous or present job.

Building Vocabulary

exercise 3

The words and phrases below are often used to describe positive personal characteristics. In small groups, discuss their meanings. Add to the list other words or phrases you might use to describe people who are successful in school or work.

concerned about other people _____

creative _____

disciplined _____

enthusiastic _____

hard-working _____

a good sense of humor _____

self-confident _____

trustworthy _____

WHAT DO YOU THINK?

Implying Qualities

One way to write about an accomplishment is to *imply*—that is, suggest indirectly—that you have certain qualities such as intelligence, honesty, and humor. You can demonstrate that you have these qualities by describing your experiences and what you have learned or accomplished by them. This way, the reader will infer that you have a particular quality. If you show how you solved a difficult problem, for example, the reader can make the inference that you are smart and creative.

Practice thinking up ways to imply particular qualities. Work with a partner. Together, think of situations that might lead a reader to infer the following qualities in a person:

intelligence courage humor patience honesty creativity

In small groups, choose three of the people below and discuss how their experiences show that they have characteristics that are important to success in work and school.

1. Miguel's mother works afternoons, so he has taken care of his younger brother after school for the last four years.
2. Yoshi taught himself how to play the guitar and plays in a band.
3. Greta works as a salesclerk in her uncle's store.
4. Shenner has been studying English for the last nine months with money he got from a scholarship as the top student in his class.
5. Paulo likes to create computer games.
6. Ana is a bicyclist and takes long trips on her bicycle.
7. Sophia has been raising three children for the last eight years.
8. All of Parvin's friends tell her their problems.

Discuss one or two experiences you could write about on a job or college application form. How does the experience show you have qualities that are important for success?

 **exercise 6** Write notes about the experience you think best shows that you have accomplished or learned something. Answer these questions:

1. What did you do?
2. What was difficult in the experience?
3. How did you face the difficulty?
4. What did the experience teach you?
5. What qualities does the experience show you have?
6. What did you accomplish through the experience?

2. Organizing Ideas
Limiting Information

 **exercise 1** Look at the beginning of the following first draft of a personal description. The writer hasn't limited what he wants to say. Is it easy to read? Cross out the information he should leave out.

> I have learned a lot working as a messenger in New York City. First of all, I have learned to persevere when there are difficulties. I also find math very difficult, but I have a tutor now who has been a great help to me. So many times I have wanted to quit, but I have tried to keep my sense of humor. I have had problems with drivers who almost run me over, constant rain for weeks at a time, unreadable addresses, and rude customers. I think the drivers in New York are the worst in any city I have seen. I have also learned that even the most routine job can be interesting.

 **exercise 2** Look at the notes you made in Exercise 6 above. Cross out any information that does not demonstrate what you have accomplished or learned.

 **exercise 3** You will probably be able to write about your experience in one paragraph. However, if the experience has several parts, you might want to use two paragraphs. For example, you might write in one paragraph about how you worked when your job was starting, and in the second paragraph about how you changed to face a problem you were experiencing. Look at your notes again. Do you think you will write everything in one paragraph or two? (You may change your mind after you begin writing.)

Writing Topic Sentences

> The topic sentence for your paragraph should make the reader interested
> in you. It should show how you're special and should be positive,
> focusing on your good points.

 These are topic sentences some students wrote for their paragraphs. Discuss them in small groups. Which ones do you like? Why?

1. I have always danced just for fun, but I recently realized that dancing has been an important learning experience for me.
2. I guess a lot of people take care of their children, so it isn't very special.
3. Two years ago, my family and I immigrated to Vancouver, Canada, and my life changed.
4. A very important thing has been happening.
5. Although I was born in Vietnam, I have been living in a small town in Texas for the last three years, and the two cultures have affected me in many important ways.
6. My relationship with my children has developed my creativity, discipline, and sense of humor.
7. Last year I had a very bad experience.
8. I like to go dancing a lot.

Writing Concluding Sentences

> The kind of paragraph you will write needs a concluding sentence. It can
> tell what you learned about yourself from the experience you chose, or it
> can describe a hope for the future. It should leave the reader with a
> positive feeling.

 These are examples of good concluding sentences. Discuss them in small groups. Why are they good?

1. I hope that my experience raising my own children will help me be a better teacher.
2. I feel that I've experienced the best of both cultures, and I hope to use this experience in my future work.
3. Now I know that if I enjoy something and know it is important, I can work really hard to make it a success.

These are examples of poor concluding sentences. In small groups, discuss why they are poor.

1. I never want to go through such a horrible experience again.
2. I guess raising children isn't easy for anyone.
3. I can never do things I don't enjoy, but when I like something I work pretty hard at it.

exercise **7**

In small groups, tell the other students what experience you are going to write about. Discuss some possible concluding sentences you might use.

3. Developing Cohesion and Style

Using the Correct Tense: Past Versus Present Perfect

Guidelines for Choosing Past or Present Perfect

PAST TENSE

Shows *completion* of action, state, time, or relevance of event, especially when the past time is mentioned.

> *example:* I was in Boston for Christmas vacation in 1986. (The time is completed and is mentioned.)

PRESENT PERFECT TENSE

Shows *incompletion* of action, state, time, or relevance of event, especially when the exact time of the past action is not important.

> *example:* I **have gone** to Boston for Christmas vacation many times. (Exactly when is not important).
> Every year since 1986 I **have gone** to Boston for Christmas vacation. (I still go.)

Choose the correct tense of the verb, past or present perfect, for these sentences. To choose, ask yourself the questions, "Is the action, state, time, or relevance of the event completed or not? Is the past time mentioned?"

examples: (You live in Detroit.) I _have lived_ (live) in Detroit for

three years.

(You live in Seattle.) I _lived_ (live) in Detroit for

three years.

1. (You've just discovered that your wallet is missing.) I _____ (lost) my wallet!

2. (You're reporting your missing wallet at a movie theater.)

   I _____ (lost) my wallet during the last show.

3. I _____ (have) two jobs this year.

4. I _____ (have) two jobs last year.

5. (You have immigrated.) I _____ (learn) a lot when I was waiting to immigrate.

6. I _____ (learn) a lot in my life.

7. I _____ (work) in this store for a month now.

8. I _____ (work) in a store for a month, but then I quit.

Using the Correct Tense: Present Perfect Versus Present Perfect Continuous

Guidelines for Choosing Present Perfect or Present Perfect Continuous

PRESENT PERFECT

The present perfect tense describes actions or situations that happened at an *unspecified* time in the past.

> *example:* I have been to San Francisco. (The time is not specified.)

The present perfect tense also describes *repeated past* actions. The following time expressions often appear with the present perfect tense: *already, just, recently, still, yet, twice, three (four, etc.) times.*

> *examples:* I have visited San Francisco three times.
> My parents have just returned from Europe.

PRESENT PERFECT CONTINUOUS

The present perfect continuous tense describes actions or situations that began in the past and have continued to the present or are still true in the present. This tense emphasizes *continuous* or *ongoing* activity; the following time expressions often appear with it: *so far, up to now, for* (+ a period of time), or *since* (+ a beginning time).

> *examples:* I have been going to that restaurant for months.
> We have been swimming a lot this summer.

PRESENT PERFECT VERSUS PRESENT PERFECT CONTINUOUS

With nonaction verbs—verbs that express feelings, opinions, possession, or perceptions—use the present perfect tense to describe actions or situations that began in the past and have continued to the present or are still true in the present. The following are examples of different kinds of nonaction verbs:

Feelings or Opinions: *be, believe, know, like, need, prefer, seem, realize, want.*
Possession: *belong to, have, own, possess*
Perceptions: *wear, smell, look, taste, see*

examples: They have known about this meeting since last month.
I haven't seen her for years.

A few verbs, such as *live, make, study, think,* and *work,* are used with the present perfect continuous or the present perfect with little difference in meaning when a time expression is used.

examples: She has worked at this company for five years.
She has been working at this company for five years.
We have lived here since 1993.
We have been living here since 1993.

Choose the correct tense, present perfect or present perfect continuous. First ask if the verb is nonaction. If it is an action verb, ask if the sentence stresses continuous or ongoing action.

examples: I <u>have known</u> (know) about this for a long time.

I <u>have been thinking</u> (think) about this since yesterday.

1. He _____ (work) with me since 1988—we still work together at the same place.

2. Has he ever _____ (work) in a restaurant?

3. I _____ (not write) my essay yet.

4. I usually write every day, but I _____ (not write) much lately.

5. She _____ already _____ (fill out) her application.

6. She _____ (fill out) her application for the last four hours.

Complete these paragraphs with the simple past, present perfect, or present perfect continuous forms of the verbs in parentheses.

I _____ (like) to write since I _____ (be) five years
  1   2
old. When I first _____ (hold) a pen in my hand and carefully
                        3
_____ (draw) the beautiful Japanese characters, I _____
         4   5
(know) I _____ (want) to be a writer. Ever since that day I
              6
_____ (write) in my free time. When I _____ (come) to
         7   8
Miami six months ago to study English, I _____ (not realize) I
                                                          9
would feel so frustrated. I _____ (have) the thoughts of a nineteen-
                                      10
year-old but the skills of a three-year-old!

Although I _____ (study) hard since that day, I still
                11
_____ (not write) an essay in English I can be proud of. This expe-
    12
rience _____ (be) frustrating, but I _____ (learn) a lot
              13   14
from it. For six months, I _____ (experience) the world through the
                                    15
words of another culture. I _____ (learn) different ways of commu-
                                        16
nicating and can use these new methods in my writing in Japanese.

Checking for Correct Tense

Exercises 1, 2, and 3 in this section give you a lot of practice with verb tenses. When you are writing a paragraph under pressure in a testing situation, take time to make sure each verb form is in the correct tense. After you've finished writing, reread your paragraph from the beginning. First, make sure the overall time frame is correct; for example, if you're talking about a past event, most verbs in the paragraph should be in some form of the past. Then, locate the verb in each sentence. Is it in the correct form? Also, look for time expressions in each sentence (such as *since* or *for*) that might require a particular tense.

Using Demonstratives to Unify a Paragraph

> A good writer uses phrases with *this, that, these,* or *those*—demonstratives—to refer to ideas in previous sentences.

 **exercise 4**   Underline the phrases with demonstratives in Exercise 3 on pages 59 and 60. What words or ideas do they refer to?

exercise 5   Complete these sentences with *this, that, these,* or *those.* Use *this* or *these* to refer to ideas or events in the present or recent past. Use *that* or *those* to refer to ideas or events farther in the past.

1. I first began to play soccer when I was four years old, and I have spent some of my happiest moments since _____ time on the soccer field.

2. A very important holiday in China is New Year's. On _____ day, we have a big feast.

3. My favorite aunt died recently. _____ experience was sad and frightening because no one close to me had ever died before. However, it has made me see life differently.

4. I have learned French, Hungarian, and Spanish, and I'm now learning English. I love the different qualities of each of _____ languages.

 **exercise 6**   Prepositional phrases with demonstratives often appear at the beginning of sentences to unify a paragraph. Add one of the following phrases to the second sentence in each of the numbered items. Use a demonstrative in each phrase. The first one is done as an example.

for _____ reason   on _____ day   in _____ city

in _____ school   because of _____ factors   during _____ years

1. Two years and six months ago, my first child was born. My life changed.

   Two years and six months ago, my first child was born. On that day, my
   life changed.

2. I lived in Thailand from the age of seven to eleven. My parents' only hope was going to live in America.

_____

_____

3. I have always been shy. Learning a new language is a challenge for me.

_____

_____

4. I came to Miami two years ago. I have had many new experiences.

_____

_____

5. However, I was too short and was not thin enough. I could not continue to dance professionally.

_____

_____

6. I came to the International English Program six months ago. I have made many new friends.

_____

_____

4. Writing the First Draft

> Write your paragraph about your personal accomplishment. You can use the ideas you wrote in the beginning of the chapter if you wish, as well as your topic sentence and concluding sentence. You can also use the demonstratives _this, that, these,_ and _those_ to unify your paragraph. Write on every other line so you can revise your paragraph easily.

5. Editing Practice
Omitting Unimportant Ideas

exercise **1**

Read the paragraph on the next page. The writer has a lot of good ideas, but some of the ideas aren't important or don't give new information. Cross out the information she should leave out. If possible, combine repetitive ideas to make the paragraph shorter.

I have been taking an English class for the last six months. This has meant a rewarding but difficult change in my life. Before that I spent all my time raising my family, a daughter who is now five and a son who is three. My daughter's name is Karen. She is in kindergarten and my son now goes to day-care. Because I did not speak much English, my focus was my home and my neighborhood, where I felt comfortable and could speak Spanish. I spoke only Spanish at home and in my neighborhood. When I needed to take my children to the doctor or speak with my landlord, my younger sisters translated for me. One of them would go with me and speak to the doctor in English and then tell me what he said in Spanish. Now I have become more independent. I have learned a lot from my classmates and I have also realized that as a mother I have had many

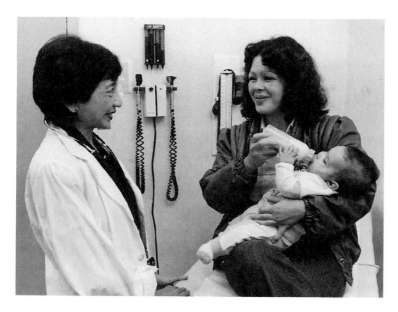

experiences that they are interested in. Now my sisters tell me to speak to the doctor or landlord myself. I go to stores where I have to speak English and I speak English in the clinic where I take my son to the doctor. This was very difficult at first, but I have been feeling more and more comfortable about my ability to communicate with other English speakers. I hope to use this new confidence to get a job.

Using Correct Capitalization

Review the rules for capitalization in Appendix Two. Correct the capitalization in these sentences if necessary.

1. Because my Mother doesn't speak english, I have to translate for her.
2. When I first moved to the southwest, I got a job as a Salesman.
3. I have lived in miami, Los Angeles, and dallas.

4. I received a Scholarship from Grant college in the Spring and started classes in september.
5. This semester I am taking Math, physics, english, and Government.

Using Correct Verb Forms

All the underlined words and phrases in the following paragraph contain errors. Correct the mistakes.

I have been worked since I have had nine years old, and I like to work. When I was having nine, we was in El Salvador and we was very poor. I pick coffee with my mother and brothers. It was hard work to carry the heavy coffee bags, which had weighed as much as one hundred pounds, up and down hills. But I learned to work with other people. For the last two years I been working as a gardener in the United States. Many people want me to come and work in their gardens, and I have learn a lot about Americans. I have even learn to speak some English. I like my job because it's different every day, and I can be outdoors.

6. Editing Your Writing

Edit your paragraph using the checklist below. First, check your paragraph for content, organization, cohesion and style using items 1, 2, and 3 in the checklist. Then edit your paragraph for grammar and form using items 4 and 5.

Editing Checklist

1. Content
   a. Does your paragraph describe your best qualities?
   b. Does it show that you can be successful in what you do?
   c. Does it let the reader infer what your best qualities are?
2. Organization
   a. Do you have too many ideas for one paragraph? Should you divide your paragraph into two paragraphs?
   b. Are there any ideas not relevant to the topic?
   c. Is your topic sentence positive? Does it make the reader want to find out more about you?
   d. Does each sentence add a new idea? Should you take out or combine repetitive sentences?
   e. Does your concluding sentence tell something you've learned or something you hope for in the future?

3. Cohesion and Style
    a. Have you used verb tenses correctly?
    b. Can you add demonstratives (*this, that, these, those*) and preposi-
       tional phrases with demonstratives to unify your paragraph?
4. Grammar
    a. Are your verb forms correct?
    b. Have you used run-on sentences or sentence fragments?
    c. Have you used plural and singular demonstratives correctly?
5. Form
    a. Is your capitalization correct?
    b. Is your spelling of past participles correct?

Exchange papers with another classmate and edit each other's paragraphs. Circle or underline in pencil any words, phrases, or sentences that you don't understand or that you think need to be corrected. Then return your paragraphs. Discuss any questions you have with your partner.

7. Writing the Second Draft

After you edit your paragraph, rewrite it neatly, using good handwriting and correct form.

A STEP beyond

Pretend to interview another student for a job or school. First find out what school or job she or he would like to apply for. Read her or his reply and ask for more information about the accomplishment. Then ask other questions, such as:

1. Why did you choose your major field of study?
2. What subjects in school have you liked the most/least? Why?
3. Tell me about your duties in past jobs.
4. Have you ever done any volunteer work? What kind and why?
5. Why are you interested in this position/school?
6. Where do you see yourself in five years?

Write a recommendation based on your interview and the accomplishment your partner wrote about. What qualities does she or he demonstrate? Would you hire or accept this person? Why or why not?

Answer these questions about your writing:

1. What have you learned so far in this course?
2. How do you feel about writing?
3. What do you like most about writing?
4. What do you like least about writing?

activity 4

Look in your school or city library for instructions on how to complete job and college applications. Following the instructions, fill out a sample application and have your classmates or teacher check it. Pay special attention to spelling, neat handwriting, and capitalization. Follow all directions carefully.

activity 5

Some applications ask for an autobiography or a personal history. Expand the paragraph you wrote for this section into an autobiography. Don't just list events in your life. Explain why they were important and what you learned from them. Finish the autobiography with a paragraph describing your future goals.

Journal Writing

activity 6

Write in your journal about one or more of these topics.

1. Write about a person you respect. Write about the qualities or experiences of that person that make you respect him or her.
2. List some of your classmates' names. Try to think of an adjective that describes him or her that begins with the same letter as his or her name, for example: trustworthy Tuan, aggressive Abu, wonderful Wan.
3. Write about a job you'd love to have.

CHAPTER **five**

Lifestyles

in this chapter

You will write an anecdote, a short description of an experience that taught you a lesson.

1. Exploring Ideas

Discussing Lessons People Learn from Experience

exercise 1

Read the following list of "lessons"—things that people might learn from experience. In small groups, discuss the list. Do you agree with all of the lessons? Try to think of experiences that might teach someone each of the lessons.

It's important to think for yourself.
Self-discipline is an essential quality.
Sometimes you have to take risks in order to get something you want.
Friendship is one of the most valuable things in life.
You should never make promises you can't keep.
If you want a good relationship, you have to compromise.
Sometimes parents really do know best.
Sometimes it's best to lie to the people you love.
Hard work can be satisfying.
The only thing that's certain is change.
It's great to be independent.

Boy! Life sure will be different....

Well... *But then again....*

My own place...

Don't worry...

exercise 2

Make up a story for one of the pictures to show how the experience taught a lesson.

Think of an experience that taught you a lesson and write about it. The lesson might be one from the list in Exercise 1 or it might be another lesson. Write the lesson in a sentence at the top of a piece of paper and draw a line under it. Then write for ten minutes about the experience that taught you that lesson. Don't worry about correctness or organization now.

WHAT DO YOU THINK?

Analyzing the Moral of a Story

Analyzing the moral—or lesson—of a story is a useful critical thinking skill. Practice this skill with a partner. Take turns telling a story. It can be a fairy tale, a fable, a children's story, or a story from religious literature. Don't tell the moral of the tale—let your partner guess. When you have finished, talk about *how* the story teaches a lesson by answering these questions: Who is the main character? What is he or she like? What happens to the main character? Does he or she change? How?

Building Vocabulary

Add to this list the new words you learned in your discussion or the words you used in your writing.

NOUNS		VERBS	ADJECTIVES
decision	_____	compromise	essential
friendship	_____	lie	valuable
importance	_____	take risks	independent
promise	_____	_____	certain
self-discipline	_____	_____	_____
change	_____	_____	_____
_____		_____	_____

Is it possible to use any of the words in the list on page 69—or different forms of the words—as different parts of speech? Make a list of the parts of speech on a separate page. Use your dictionary to help you.

examples:

Noun	Verb	Adjective
importance	—	important
change	change	changing

2. Organizing Ideas
Understanding Anecdotes

An anecdote is a short description of something that really happened. Writers use anecdotes to illustrate or explain ideas. Many anecdotes or stories do not have topic sentences because they are organized chronologically rather than according to topic.

You are going to write an anecdote about something that happened to you that taught you a lesson about life. Your anecdote should answer these questions:

1. *When* and *where* did the story take place?
2. *Who* was involved and *what* was their relationship?
3. *What* happened?
4. *Why* did it happen?
5. *What* was the result?

Read the anecdote that follows and discuss it with your classmates. Does it answer all the preceding questions? Which questions does most of the story answer? Which questions does it answer in the first two sentences? Which does it answer in the last sentence?

One summer weekend some friends and I decided to walk to a waterfall we had heard about. Since it was too far to walk along the road, we followed a railroad line. We had walked five or six miles when we came to a high rock wall where the tracks entered a tunnel. This tunnel didn't look very long, but it was narrow and we knew it would be dangerous if a train came. However, we couldn't climb the rocks or walk around them and no one wanted to go back. Finally we decided to go through. I knew it was foolish, but I went because the others did.

As soon as we entered the tunnel, we saw that it was longer and darker than we had thought. Suddenly everyone was frightened and we all began to run. "This is crazy!" I thought. We ran faster and it got lighter in the tunnel. Then we were outside and we fell on the ground gasping. About a minute later a train came through. That was when I finally realized the importance of thinking for myself.

focus on testing

Checking for Chronological Order

As you've just seen, an important part of writing an anecdote is organizing events in chronological order. When you write an anecdote in a timed testing situation, plan before you write. Start by listing the events in your story on a piece of scratch paper. Then check your list: Is everything in the right order? Is the order logical? If not, move things around or delete them. Are there any gaps? If so, fill in any missing information. Then use your list to write the paragraph.

Writing Anecdotes

When writing an anecdote, you might begin a new paragraph for several different reasons. Here are some of them:

1. The time or place of the story changes.
2. You begin to tell about a new person.
3. Something important happens in the story.
4. You stop telling the story and explain something about it.

In the anecdote about the tunnel, what was the writer's reason for starting a new paragraph when he wrote "As soon as we entered the tunnel . . ."?

_____

_____

Using Details

Your anecdote will be more interesting if you can make the reader "live" the experience with you. One way to do this is by using details to help the reader see what you saw and feel what you felt. Here is the second paragraph of the tunnel anecdote without the details that make it seem more real. What details did the writer leave out?

> We started to walk through the tunnel, but then we got frightened and started to run. After we got outside a train came through. That was when I finally realized the importance of thinking for myself.

One difficulty with details is that they can easily become *digressions:*

> One summer weekend some friends and I decided to walk to a waterfall we had heard about. This waterfall was called Horsetail Falls because it looked like a horse's tail. There was a place to swim at the bottom and it was a wonderful place for a picnic . . .

In a good anecdote, everything leads to the conclusion. If a detail leads away from the lesson (even if it is true and interesting), take it out of your anecdote.

exercise **3**

Here are the writer's notes for part of the tunnel anecdote. In small groups, discuss the questions that follow.

didn't look very long	a lot of bushes, more rocks
narrow, dangerous	on right
rocks 80–100 ft. high—	couldn't go right or left
couldn't climb them	no trains all day—maybe
river on left	tracks not used?

1. Which details did the writer leave out of the anecdote?
2. Do you agree with his decisions?

3. Developing Cohesion and Style

Using the Past Perfect Tense

In the anecdote about the tunnel, everything happened in the past. The writer used mainly simple past tense verbs to tell the story in the order that it happened. But three times the writer looked back in time and used the past perfect tense to write about events that *had happened earlier.*

Interactions Two • Writing

exercise 1 Find the three sentences in the anecdote that used the past perfect tense. Parts of these sentences are listed under 1, 2, and 3 in the chart below. What event happened *earlier* in each sentence? What happened *later*? Complete the chart. Part of number 1 is done as an example.

in the anecdote	happened earlier	happened later
1. We _decided_ to walk to a waterfall we _____ about.		We decided to walk to a waterfall.
2. We _____ five or six miles when we _____ to a high rock wall.		
3. We _____ that it was longer and darker than we _____ .		

exercise 2 The following passage is an early draft of the tunnel anecdote. (You will notice that it still has a lot of digressions.) Fill in the blanks with the simple past tense or the past perfect tense of the verbs in parentheses.

One summer weekend some friends and I decided to take a picnic to a waterfall we had heard about. Some people _____ (drive) cars and _____ (take) the food, but the rest of us _____ (want) to walk. Since it was too far to walk along the road, we followed a railroad line. We had walked five or six miles when we came to a high rock wall where the tracks entered a tunnel. We _____ (be) surprised. Nobody _____ (tell) us about it. The tunnel didn't look very long, but it was narrow and we knew it would be dangerous if a train came. However, we couldn't climb the rocks or go around them, and no one wanted to go back. I _____ (have) a good breakfast, but some of the others _____ (not eat). They _____ (want) to get to the waterfall and have lunch. Finally we decided to go through. I knew it was foolish, but I went because the others did.

As soon as we entered the tunnel, we saw that it was longer and darker than we had thought. Earlier we _____ (decide) to walk and to stay

₉

together, but suddenly everyone was frightened and we all began to run. "This is crazy," I thought. "Why didn't I go back?" We ran faster and it got lighter in the tunnel. Then we were outside and we fell on the ground gasping. No one

_____ (fall) in the tunnel. We _____ (be) all safe. About

₁₀   ₁₁

a minute later a train came through.

We _____ (be) upset because we _____ (come) so

₁₂   ₁₃

close to death. We _____ also angry with ourselves for being so

₁₄

foolish. Later we _____ (hear) that two boys _____ (die)

₁₅   ₁₆

in that tunnel the month before. That was when I finally realized the importance of thinking for myself.

exercise 3 Reread the paragraph above and decide which sections are digressions and should be omitted. Cross them out.

4. Writing the First Draft

> Now you are ready to write your own anecdote. Use the experience you wrote about earlier or choose another experience. Be sure to choose one that taught you a clear lesson. Write on every other line so you can revise your paragraph easily.

5. Editing Practice
Omitting Digressions and Unimportant Details

exercise 1 The following paragraph is the first part of an anecdote. The last sentence of the anecdote will be, "That was when I learned the satisfaction of doing hard work well." Revise the paragraph by taking out digressions and details that do not lead to the lesson of the anecdote. Use one line to cross them out. (You don't have to fix the grammar after you do this.)

The year I was fifteen my parents sent me to work on my uncle's farm for the summer. It was in South Carolina and they had peach trees, and cows and chickens. They didn't make much money and my father was always telling my uncle to sell the farm and come to Chicago. I didn't want to go and I didn't like it when I got there. It was very hot and muggy most of the time. My cousins got up at 4:30 in the morning and went to bed at 9:00 at night and in between they worked. I had never worked on a farm before, and my cousin Wayne had to teach me everything, like milking the cows, driving the tractor, and so on. We were the same age, but I was bigger than he was. I was already six feet tall. Even so I couldn't do anything as well as he could. I had a lot of friends at home and we always hung around together, especially in summer. I used to think about them. "They don't have to work on some dumb farm," I thought. "How come I have to?"

 Compare your revision to your classmates' work. Did you take out the same things?

exercise 3 The following paragraph is a continuation of the story. Correct the underlined verbs if they are wrong.

I'm there about two weeks when Wayne and I have to load some bales of hay. After half an hour we loaded a lot of bales and it was getting hard to throw them up onto the wagon. "I'm going to miss the next one," I thought. But Wayne missed first. His bale didn't go high enough and it has fallen back down. I took a deep breath and throw mine. I did it! "Hey Dad!" Wayne called. "Did you see that?" I did it again and they cheer. I felt wonderful. After that everything change. Wayne and I were friends and we enjoy competing with each other in everything. Usually he was better, but sometimes I am. I worked hard all summer and I love it. I learn a lot that summer, but the most important lesson is that day in the hayfield. That was when I learn the satisfaction of doing hard work well.

6. Editing Your Writing

 Edit your anecdote using the checklist below. First, check your paragraph for content, organization, cohesion, and style using items 1, 2, and 3 in the checklist. Then edit your paragraph for grammar and form using items 4 and 5.

Editing Checklist

1. Content
   a. Is your story interesting?
   b. Does the lesson (conclusion) fit the story you told?
   c. Have you given enough information?
2. Organization
   a. Have you avoided unimportant details and digressions?
   b. Have you used paragraph divisions to make the story clearer?
3. Cohesion and Style
   a. Have you used transition words correctly?
   b. Are your sentences in logical order?
4. Grammar
   a. Have you used the past, present perfect, and past perfect tenses correctly?
5. Form
   a. Did you use correct paragraph format? (indentation, division of words between syllables, margins)
   b. Did you use correct punctuation? (capitalization, commas, periods)
   c. Did you check the spelling of the words you are not sure of?

 Exchange papers with another classmate and edit each other's anecdotes. Circle or underline in pencil any words, phrases, or sentences that you don't understand or that you think need to be corrected. Then return your anecdotes. Discuss any questions you have with your partner.

7. Writing the Second Draft

> After you edit your anecdote, rewrite it neatly, using good handwriting and correct form. Give your anecdote to your teacher for comments.

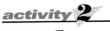 Read the anecdotes of two of your classmates. Then answer these questions about each anecdote.

1. What exactly made the anecdote interesting for you? Be specific. You can mention the incidents, some of the details, the lesson, or something else.
2. Do you agree with the student's conclusion (lesson) or not? Briefly explain why or why not.

 Write down the story you discussed in the What Do You Think? activity on page 69 (or you can write another story that teaches a lesson or has a moral). Be sure to include the moral of the story at the end. Form small groups, and read each other's stories. Are any of the stories similar? If your group has students from different countries, are there similar stories in those countries? Which story was the most interesting? Why? If you like, collect all the stories and make copies for all your classmates to read.

Journal Writing

 Write in your journal about one or more of the following topics.

1. Write about a frustrating day or experience you've had recently.
2. Write about the thing that makes you most angry.
3. Write about the thing that makes you most happy.

CHAPTER six

The Global Village

in this chapter

You are going to write a paragraph about the effects of the global village on your life.

STEPS TO writing

1. Exploring Ideas

Marshall McLuhan (1911–1980) was a Canadian professor and writer interested in modern communications. In his 1967 book *Understanding Media,* McLuhan wrote that "the new electronic interdependence recreates the world in the image of the global village." At that time, McLuhan was referring to how television allowed people all over the world to share information. With the introduction of new technologies such as satellite dishes, personal computers, and electronic mail, McLuhan's idea of the "global village" seems more true now than ever.

Marshall McLuhan

Expanding a Definition

 What does the phrase *global village* mean to you? Discuss it in small groups.

 Look at the pictures below and on page 81. Can you think of another example of the global village?

Building Vocabulary

Here are some words that you may be able to use in your writing. Did you use any others in your discussion? If so, add them to the list.

ADJECTIVES	NOUNS	VERBS
isolated	multiculturalism	import
cosmopolitan	resources	export
multinational	diversity	influence
transnational	telecommunications	
technological	market	_____
	immigrant	_____
	tourism	_____
_____		_____
_____	_____	_____
_____	_____	_____
_____	_____	_____

Defining Terms

It's important to define certain terms when you want to use them in a discussion or essay because they can mean different things to different people. One way to define a word is to give an example. Practice this by reading the following words. Work with a partner, and take turns defining each one by giving an example. (You can look them up in the dictionary, but be prepared to explain what they mean to *you*, in your own words, because this is what you will have to do in a discussion or in writing.)

multiculturalism   diversity   global village   interdependence

2. Organizing Ideas

Listing Information

exercise 1   You are going to write about how the shrinking world affects your everyday life. Think about the good and bad effects of the global village. In the chart below, list them in the proper columns.

GOOD EFFECTS   **BAD EFFECTS**

_____   _____

_____   _____

_____   _____

Clustering

Clustering is one way to help you organize your ideas. It can help you decide what to focus on when a topic is very broad. To make a cluster diagram, write the topic on a piece of paper. Then write all your ideas about the topic around the paper. Connect the ideas that are related (go together). Look at the example on the top of page 83.

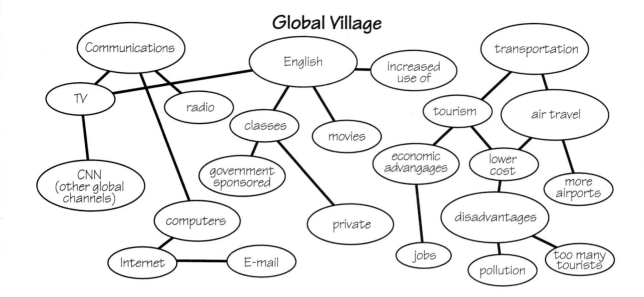

Global Village

Communications — TV — CNN (other global channels)

Communications — radio

Communications — classes — government sponsored — computers — Internet — E-mail

English — increased use of

English — classes — private

English — movies

transportation — tourism — air travel — more airports

tourism — economic advangages — jobs

tourism — lower cost

lower cost — disadvantages — pollution — too many tourists

exercise  2

Make your own cluster diagram. First, get all of your ideas down on paper. Then, see which ideas are related and connect them.

exercise  3

Look at your cluster diagram and think about which ideas would make a good paragraph. Draw a circle around the part of the diagram (group of ideas) you want to write about. Use these questions to help you decide which ideas to choose.

- Is the information interesting?
- Are the different ideas clearly related?
- Do you have enough information for a paragraph?
- Can you limit the information to one paragraph?

focus on testing

Diagramming Your Ideas

In Organizing Ideas, you practiced clustering. This, and other kinds of diagrams can help you save time when you are writing under pressure. Take a few minutes *before* you start writing in a testing situation to diagram your ideas. You can draw a cluster, or any other kind of diagram, such as a flow chart, that works for you. This will help you organize your ideas and see how they are related before you write.

3. Developing Cohesion and Style

Choosing the Correct Part of Speech

> When you write a paragraph or longer composition, you have to be careful to use the correct forms of words that have different forms for different parts of speech.

exercise  Complete this chart with the correct forms of these words. Use your dictionary to help you. The first one is done as an example. (More than one noun form may be possible.)

NOUNS	VERBS	ADJECTIVES	ADVERBS
isolation or isolationist	isolate	isolated	XXXXXXX
multiculturalism	XXXXXXX	_____	_____
interdependence	XXXXXXX	_____	XXXXXXX
_____ or _____	import	_____	XXXXXXX
_____ or _____	export	_____	XXXXXXX
_____	_____	diverse	_____
_____	influence	_____	_____
technology	XXXXXXX	_____	_____
market	_____	XXXXXXX	XXXXXX
_____ or _____	immigrate	XXXXXXX	XXXXXXX
_____ or _____	_____	touristy	XXXXXXX

**exercise 2**   Complete each sentence with the correct part of speech of the word in parentheses.

1. Many countries are worried about increasing _____ (immigrate) and have strict laws to control the number of people who can become citizens.

2. _____ (touristy) is an important source of revenue for a lot of countries.

3. Many cities in the United States have a _____ (multiculturism) atmosphere. This can easily be seen in the great _____ (diverse) of ethnic restaurants.

4. The world is truly becoming _____ (interdependence). No country today can survive in _____ (isolate).

5. Laws which limit the _____ (import) of certain products are necessary to help local industries grow.

6. It is almost impossible to keep up with all the recent _____ (technology) changes.

Using Relative Clauses

The relative pronouns *who, which, where,* and *that* can be used to introduce relative clauses. The relative clauses are underlined in the examples below.

examples	notes
The woman *who / that* runs the restaurant is Japanese.	*Who* refers to people.
The watch *that / which* I bought you is Swiss.	*Which* refers to things. *That* refers to people and things.
The office *where* I work employs people from four different countries.	*Where* refers to places.

**exercise 3**   Complete these five sentences with the correct relative pronouns.

1. The global village has arrived, and people _____ do not realize this are going to be left behind.

2. The use of computers, _____ now link not only governments but individuals all over the world, has broken down national borders.

3. The global village is a place _____ many languages are spoken; however, the one _____ is predominant is English.

4. Parts for the car _____ I just bought were made in six different countries.

5. Some futurists foresee the world as city-states _____ are connected by technology.

Using Specific Examples

 Read these two paragraphs. Then work with a partner and answer these questions about the paragraphs. Which one is more interesting? Why?

1. People often say that the world is getting smaller, and I believe that this is true. However, it is not only getting smaller, it is becoming more homogenous. People are moving from place to place. In the small town where I live, you can eat in restaurants from several different countries. The neighborhood school has children from many different language backgrounds. We can watch television in different languages too. In addition, I drive a foreign car, have an imported television, VCR, and camera. Last of all, most of my clothes were made overseas.

2. This is a typical day in the "global village" where I live. My Japanese clock radio wakes me up. I dress in my T-shirt, which was made in Thailand, and my jeans, which were made in Taiwan. I walk out into a Spanish-named street full of German cars. I go for breakfast at a Mexican cafe run by a Japanese woman and then stop at the Korean grocery store. Back home, I can listen to the news in Spanish, Chinese, Japanese, Arabic, Korean, or Hindi. My wife's school has parent-teacher association meetings that look like a mini United Nations. Where is this multicultural paradise? In California, but it could be in many other places. The world is looking more and more like the United States, but the United States is also looking more and more like the rest of the world.

 **exercise 5** Look at your cluster diagram and the notes you made for your paragraph. Do you need more examples? Add them.

4. Writing the First Draft

> Write your paragraph using the organization you worked out at the beginning of this chapter. Write on every other line so that you can revise your paragraph easily.

5. Editing Practice
Punctuating Relative Clauses

> There are two different types of relative clauses: restrictive and nonrestrictive.
>
> • A restrictive relative clause tells you which person, place, or thing the writer is referring to. The information in the restrictive relative clause is necessary to complete the sentence. Don't use commas with restrictive clauses.
>
> *examples:*   Children *who are bilingual* have an advantage over their monolingual playmates.
>   May and October are the months that *I like best*.

Note that if you omit the restrictive relative clauses *who are bilingual* (example 1) and *that I like best* (example 2), the sentences are incomplete.

- A nonrestrictive relative clause gives additional information. This additional information is not necessary to complete the sentence. In nonrestrictive clauses, use *which* instead of *that* to refer to things. Use commas to separate a nonrestrictive clause from the rest of the sentence.

  examples: My brother's children, *who are bilingual,* are seven and ten years old.
  May and October, *which have the best weather,* are my favorite months.

Note that if you omit the nonrestrictive relative clauses *who are bilingual* (example 1) and *which have the best weather* (example 2), the sentences are still complete.

Do not use *that* with nonrestrictive relative clauses.

 Read these sentences and add commas where necessary.

1. The global village which was first discussed by Marshall McLuhan in the 1960s has finally come to be.

2. The teachers who teach in the global village should have a multicultural point of view.

3. My father works in a cement factory that is owned by Japanese business-men.

4. New technology which is the backbone of the global village is growing at a faster rate than ever.

5. My students who come from six different countries are very interested in learning about other places in the world.

6. World markets are controlled by huge corporations that may not care about their workers.

6. Editing Your Writing

 Edit your paragraph using the checklist on the facing page. First, check your paragraph for content, organization, cohesion and style using items 1, 2, and 3 in the checklist. Then edit your paragraph for grammar and form using items 4 and 5.

Editing Checklist

1. Content
   Does your paragraph give examples when necessary?
2. Organization
   Does your paragraph have a narrow-enough focus?
3. Cohesion and Style
   Have you used relative clauses correctly?
4. Grammar
   a. Have you used the correct part of speech for each word?
   b. Have you used relative clauses correctly?
5. Form
   a. Have you used a capital letter to begin each sentence?
   b. Have you used a period to end each sentence?
   c. Have you punctuated relative clauses correctly?

 **exercise 2** Exchange papers with another classmate and edit each other's paragraphs. Circle or underline in pencil any words, phrases, or sentences that you don't understand or that you think need to be corrected. Then return your paragraphs. Discuss any questions you have with your partner.

7. Writing the Second Draft

Rewrite your paragraph neatly, using good handwriting and correct form. Then give it to your teacher for comments.

A STEP **beyond**

 **activity 1** Find an article in a magazine or a newspaper that talks about the global village. Does the writer mention any effects that you and your classmates have not thought of?

 **activity 2** Interview classmates and/or teachers about the global village. Compile their reactions and write a composition incorporating their opinions.

activity 3

Interview an older friend or relative about how his/her world has changed in the past 30–40 years. Take notes. Then, in small groups, share your findings with other classmates.

activity 4

Have you ever heard of a time capsule? A time capsule is a group of items that can tell people in the future something about the way people live today. Some people put such items in a box or other container, close the container, and put it away. They write instructions telling people not to open it for 100 years or more.

Work in small groups. Make a list of 10 items to put in a time capsule. They should be items that will best help people in the future understand what life is like now. Brainstorm a list of items. Then discuss them and choose *only* 10 items for your capsule. When you finish, join another group and share your lists. How are your items similar? How are they different? Why did you choose these items?

Journal Writing

activity 5

Write about one or both of the following topics.

1. Write about how you think your world will change in the next 20 years. Write for 15 minutes.
2. Write about any aspect of the global village that interests you.

CHAPTER seven

North America: The Land and the People

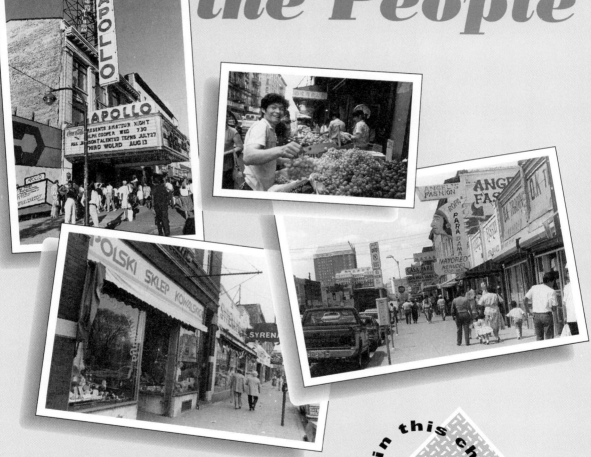

You are going to write a story about an immigrant's experiences.

1. Exploring Ideas

Interviewing Someone

exercise **1**

A great majority of the populations of the United States and Canada is made up of immigrants or descendants of immigrants. Look at this picture of immigrants taking an oath of citizenship. In small groups, discuss these questions.

Becoming U.S. citizens

1. Why do people choose to immigrate to a new country?
2. What are some of the problems that immigrants face? Make a list of the problems.

_____

_____

_____

_____

_____

_____

3. If you were going to interview an immigrant, what questions would you like to ask him or her? Make a list of possible interview questions.

You are going to write about an immigrant—yourself, someone you know, someone in your class—or you can make up a story about someone in the picture on page 92.

 Work in pairs. Interview your partner using the interview questions you just wrote. On a separate page, take notes on your partner's answers. Then your partner will interview you and take notes on your answers. When your partner interviews you, you may answer as yourself, or you may pretend you are someone you know or someone in the picture on page 92.

 Exchange notes. What else can you add to the notes your partner made?

Building Vocabulary

 In your discussion you may have heard some words you don't understand, or you may find that you don't know the English word for some of the ideas you want to express. Find out the meaning of any words you don't understand and add them to the list below.

NOUNS	VERBS	ADJECTIVES
confusion	confuse	anxious
depression	depress	confusing
excitement	emigrate	depressed
homeland	excite	exciting
humiliation	humiliate	homesick
native land	immigrate	humiliated
refugee	thrill	thrilled
thrill		upset
_____	_____	_____
_____	_____	_____
_____	_____	_____
_____	_____	_____
_____	_____	_____

Distinguishing Appropriate Topics

When you interview someone to get information for a story, it's important to know which questions are appropriate—or polite—to ask, and which are not. Knowing this depends partly on how familiar you are with the person's culture, partly on common sense, and partly on the purpose or topic of the interview. Practice distinguishing appropriate from inappropriate interview questions. Work with a partner. Read the following list of questions. Decide which questions are appropriate, and which are inappropriate, to ask in an interview about an immigrant experience in North American culture. Write "A" (appropriate) or "I" (inappropriate) next to each question. Then think of some additional appropriate questions.

_____ How old are you?

_____ When did you come to this country?

_____ How much do you weigh?

_____ What do you do for a living?

_____ How much money do you make?

_____ Where did / do you go to school?

_____ What do you think of the government of this country?

_____ What's your favorite food?

Using Verbal Adjectives to Describe Feelings

Many of the verbs that describe emotions are verbal adjectives. Verbal adjectives take two forms. One form ends in -ed. It describes the person (or animal) that has a feeling. The other form ends in -ing. It describes the person, animal, or thing that creates a feeling.

examples: Eva heard some _surprising_ news.
She was _surprised_ by the news.

Here is a list of some common verbal adjectives:

confused	excited	surprised	tired
confusing	exciting	surprising	tiring
depressed	frightened	terrified	
depressing	frightening	terrifying	
disappointed	humiliated	thrilled	
disappointing	humiliating	thrilling	

 **exercise 5**

Look at these sentences. Circle the noun phrase that the adjective in italics describes.

1. At first, the noise and crowds of the big city were *terrifying* to Ahmad.

2. Tran was *disappointed* when he couldn't find a job.

3. Living in a new country can be *confusing*.

4. Wilma was *surprised* that learning English was so easy.

 **exercise 6**

Complete these sentences with adjective forms of the words below.

excite tire surprise
thrill depress

1. Tran was _____ by American customs.

2. Amara thought working full-time and studying was _____.

3. Alain was _____ and homesick when he first moved to the United States.

4. At first, Junko thought that life in New York was _____.

5. Most people think that flying is _____.

exercise 7

Complete these sentences with verbal adjectives. Talk about your true feelings. You may want to use verbal adjectives with the same meaning as *happy, sad,* or *scary.*

1. Life in a foreign country can be _____.

2. I was _____ on the first day of class.

3. Leaving home is _____.

4. My friends and family were _____ when I left.

Write some sentences for your paragraphs, using verbal adjectives.

_____

_____

_____

_____

_____

2. Organizing Ideas
Keeping to One Subject

When you write, you should be careful to keep to the subject. All of the information that you give should be closely related to the topic of your paragraph.

Read this paragraph. Does it contain any irrelevant information? Cross out any sentences that do not belong.

When Lee Kim first arrived in the United States from Korea, he was very frightened. Suddenly, he was entering a world that was almost totally incomprehensible to him. He was living in an apartment. He was unable to obtain information he needed. Lee could not read a street sign, ask a question, or understand directions. Lee's brother spoke English well. However, Lee's life changed for the better when he decided to go to Newton Community College to take English classes. This school is located on the corner of Broad Street and First Avenue.

Developing Ideas by Adding Details

Make sure to develop your paragraph fully by adding important details. One way to do this is to think of questions that your reader might ask about your paragraph. The answers to these questions can give you more details to add to your paragraph. For example, in the paragraph about Lee Kim in Exercise 1, one question a reader might ask is: How was Lee's life changed for the better when he decided to go to Newton Community College? Answering this question would add more detail to the paragraph and develop it more fully.

 **exercise 2**   Read the following paragraph. How fully has the writer developed his or her ideas?

> Juan Ordónez had many dreams when he was young, so he decided to immigrate. He left his birthplace in 1986. When he first arrived in his new country, his life was very difficult. However, now he is much happier. Juan is glad that he decided to leave his homeland.

What questions do you still have about the topic? Write your questions on the lines below. Remember that the answers to these questions can add important details to make the paragraph more interesting.

example: What is Juan's new country?

1. _____

2. _____

3. _____

4. _____

5. _____

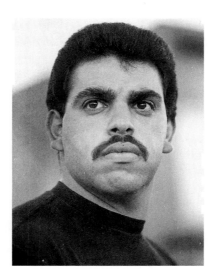

Developing Your Ideas

In Exercise 2, you practiced asking questions about a paragraph. This is a good technique to use when you have to write a paragraph for a timed test. After you write, take a few minutes to ask yourself *wh-* questions (*who, what, where, when, how,* etc.) about each sentence in your paragraph. If your sentences already answer each question, congratulations! You probably have a well-developed paragraph. If not, add sentences to develop your ideas further.

exercise **3**

In small groups, write answers to your questions, then rewrite the paragraph using the new information. The result should be an interesting, well-developed paragraph.

Dividing a Composition into Paragraphs

Your story can have two or more paragraphs. For example, the first paragraph might be about the immigrant's life in his or her native country and the second paragraph about his or her new life. You might also write one paragraph about what an immigrant's life was like upon first arriving and a second paragraph about how his or her life changed.

exercise **4**

Look at the notes you made for your story. Divide them into paragraphs. Is there any information that seems irrelevant? Is there any information you should add?

Writing Topic Sentences

A good topic sentence should capture the reader's interest and explain what the paragraph is about.

exercise **5**

Look at these topic sentences. Which ones do you like? Why? Add information to the ones you don't like to make them more interesting. Remember that there are several ways to make good topic sentences.

1. Basima never considered leaving her home before the summer of 1988.
2. Wai Fon Yu was born in Beijing.
3. Life in her native Colombia was not easy for Silvia.
4. Domingo is an immigrant from Spain.
5. His name is Walid.

exercise 6   Write a topic sentence for the first paragraph of your story.

Writing Concluding Sentences

> Although most immigrants face many problems, they usually have hope for the future. One way to conclude a story about a personal experience is with a sentence that expresses hope for the future.

exercise 7   Look at these concluding sentences. Which ones do you like the best? Why?

1. Marta is looking forward to a better future now that her family troubles are over.
2. José plans to live in Canada for the rest of his life.
3. Although Junpen is still sometimes homesick, she knows that her decision to live in the United States was the right one.
4. Mohammed is waiting for the day when he can return home.

3. Developing Cohesion and Style

Using Gerunds as Subjects

> A gerund is the *-ing* form of a verb used as a noun—for example, *moving, becoming, working.* (See the appendix for rules for spelling changes.) Gerunds or gerund phrases are sometimes subjects of sentences.
>   Look at these sentences with gerund phrases.
>
> *examples:*   *Moving* to the *United States* was the most exciting experience of Juan's life.
> *Becoming* a *Canadian citizen* made Somsak very proud.
> *Working* as a *garbage man* made Gaetano sick.

exercise 1   Make gerund phrases from the words in parentheses to write sentences in items 1–5 below.

1. (Talk about politics) was forbidden in Teresa's country

---

2. (Learn to live in a new culture) is difficult for anyone

_____

3. (Leave your homeland) is never easy

_____

4. (Live on welfare) was a humiliating experience for Samuel

_____

5. (Be away from his family) made Jaime very sad

_____

exercise  Complete these sentences with a gerund phrase.

    1. _____ for the first time is a thrilling experience.

    2. _____ made Marta very happy.

    3. _____ can be very tiring.

    4. _____ is important to Yoko.

    5. _____ was easy for Katrina.

Using Gerunds and Infinitives in Parallel Constructions

When you write, it is important to use gerunds and infinitives in parallel constructions. The gerunds and infinitives in the following sentences are parallel. The sentences are correct.

    examples: _Working_ during the day and _studying_ at night made
    (correct)   Miguel very tired.
                   When I first arrived in Toronto, I liked _to walk_ in the
                   beautiful parks and _listen_ to people speak English.

The gerunds and infinitives in these sentences are not parallel. The sentences are incorrect.

    examples: In our native country my family enjoyed _to visit_
    (incorrect)   relatives and _having_ picnics in our orchard.
                   Visiting new places and _to meet_ new people always
                   interested Shadi.

 **exercise 3**

The following paragraph includes some mistakes in the use of gerunds and infinitives. Find the mistakes and correct them.

Leaving friends and family is difficult.

A DIFFICULT DECISION

Decide to leave her country was very difficult for Berta. Unfortunately, in her native country she was unable to going to school or find a good job. When her husband suggested that they leave, she knew he was right. Visit her friends and family for the last time was the hardest thing she ever had to do. She avoided calling and tell them of the decision for a long time. She was so lonely during her first few months abroad that she thought she would die. Berta feels comfortable in her new country now, but she has never stopped loving her country and to feel homesick for the people she left behind.

Using *Would* and *Used to*

When English speakers talk about past events they often use the simple past tense. When they are talking about past habits, however, they sometimes use *would* + verb or *used to* + verb.

examples: When I was young, I *used to get up* early every morning.
When I was young, I *would get up* early every morning.

You can use *would* and *used to* to talk about repeated activities. However, for continuing states using verbs such as *have, think, live, believe,* and *own* you can use *used to* only.

examples: Her grandfather *used to have* a long white beard.
She *used to think* that he was the oldest man in the world.

Remember that you cannot use *would* and *used to* for activities that happened only once or twice or states that continued for only a short time. In these cases you must use the simple past tense.

examples: Anna *started* school when she was seven.
On the first day of school she *was* afraid because she *thought* that her mother *was leaving* her forever.

 **exercise 4**

Complete these sentences in as many ways as possible. Some sentences can take only the simple past. Others can take the simple past or *used to*. Some can take the simple past, *would,* or *used to*.

1. Marta _____ (live) in a small village in Ecuador.

2. When he was young, Alfonso _____ (visit) his grandmother every day.

3. Many immigrants _____ (believe) that anyone could get rich very quickly in the United States.

4. When Greta was fifteen, she _____ (come) to live in the United States.

5. In El Salvador, Teresa's family _____ (own) a large farm.

Many times students use *used to* too often in one paragraph. Good writers often begin with a sentence using *used to* and then continue with *would* or the simple past tense.

 **exercise 5**

Read this paragraph. Then discuss it with a partner. Do you like it? Say why or why not.

From the time he was young, Abid had to work very hard. He used to get up early in the morning to study. After he finished studying, he used to go to work in his uncle's cheese factory. Then he used to go to school for morning classes. At lunchtime he used to deliver pastries for a local bakery. Then he used to go back to school. After school, he used to have to work at his uncle's factory for a few more hours. Despite all of his hard work, Abid used to be the best student in his class.

 **exercise 6**

Rewrite the paragraph, changing *used to* to *would* or the simple past tense to make it more interesting.

exercise 7 Think about the paragraphs you are going to write about an immigrant. Write three or four sentences using *used to* or *would* that you could use in your composition.

4. Writing the First Draft

> Write your composition using the topic sentence you wrote and the notes you made. Make your paragraphs interesting by adding details. Don't worry about grammar when you write the first draft. Write on every other line so you can revise your paragraph easily.

5. Editing Practice
Adding Topic and Concluding Sentences and Omitting Irrelevant Information

exercise 1 The first paragraph of this composition needs a topic sentence, and the last paragraph needs a concluding sentence. Read the story and then add a topic sentence and a concluding sentence. Cross out any irrelevant information.

_____

_____

When Nu Phong was very young she lived in a small village in Vietnam with her parents and her brothers and sisters. Her parents were farmers. They grew rice and vegetables. Sometimes her parents would talk about the war but only a few soldiers came to Nu Phong's village, so her family felt safe. Nu Phong's older brother decided not to fight in the war. Then one day bombs began to fall on their village and many soldiers came to fight there. Nu Phong's parents died in the fighting. Nu Phong and her sister went to live with their grandmother in Saigon. One day when Nu Phong was fourteen their grandmother came and told them that they were going to go to the United States to live with their aunt.

At first, Nu Phong's life in the United States was very difficult. She went to an American high school and she felt very uncomfortable there. She went to John F. Kennedy High School in Houston, Texas. Learning English wasn't easy, and the other students were very different from her. Gradually, Nu Phong began to make friends, first with other foreign students and finally with some Americans. She learned to speak English well and became comfortable with the American way of life. Although Nu Phong still thought about her life in Vietnam, she didn't feel homesick anymore. Nu Phong's sister was still planning to return to Vietnam. Today Nu Phong is eighteen years old. When she graduates from high school, she plans to go to college to become a nurse.

_____

_____

_____

_____

Punctuating Sentences with Transitions and Subordinating Conjunctions

Remember to use transition words to connect ideas in a paragraph. Don't overuse them, however. When transition words such as *first of all, finally, in addition,* and *also* come at the beginning of a sentence, put a comma after them.

> example: At first, Nu Phong's life in the United States was very difficult.

Don't confuse subordinating conjunctions such as *when* and *because* with transition words. (See the appendix for lists of subordinating conjunctions and transition words.) Subordinating conjunctions connect dependent clauses and independent clauses within a *sentence.* Transition words connect ideas within an entire *paragraph,* in order to make it cohesive.

> *Subordinating conjunction:* I was unhappy, *so* I wanted to go home.
> *Transition word:* I couldn't speak English. I had no friends, and I was living in a terrible place. *Therefore,* I wanted to go home.

 **exercise 2**   Edit this paragraph for correct punctuation around transition words and subordinating conjunctions.

> May 14, 1981 was the most memorable day in my life. On that day, my family left our home in Iran to go to live in the United States. Although I was only eight years old I thought I knew what life would be like in America. Because I had seen many movies about life there I remember wondering if I would be able to have a horse and carry a gun. In addition even though my father kept telling me that we were going to be living in a big city, I still imagined myself in the "Wild West."

6. Editing Your Writing

 **exercise 1**   Edit your composition using the checklist below. First, check your paragraph for content, organization, cohesion, and style using items 1, 2, and 3 in the checklist. Then edit your paragraph for grammar and form using items 4 and 5.

Editing Checklist

1. Content
   a. Is the information interesting?
   b. Does the composition answer most of the reader's questions?
2. Organization
   a. Are paragraphs organized chronologically?
   b. Does your first paragraph have a good topic sentence?
   c. Does your last paragraph have a concluding sentence?
3. Cohesion and Style
   a. Are your gerund and infinitive constructions parallel?
   b. Did you use 'used to' too often?
4. Grammar
   a. Did you use *used to* and *would* correctly?
   b. Did you use verbal abjectives correctly?
5. Form
   a. Did you use correct paragraph format? (indentation, division of words between syllables, margins)
   b. Did you use correct punctuation? (capitalization, commas, periods)
   c. Did you check the spelling of the words you are not sure of?

Exchange papers with another classmate and edit each other's compositions. Circle or underline in pencil any words, phrases, or sentences that you don't understand or that you think need to be corrected. Then return your compositions. Discuss any questions you have with your partner.

7. Writing the Second Draft

> After you edit your composition, rewrite it neatly, using good handwriting and correct form. Give your composition to your teacher for comments.

 beyond

 Read your stories aloud in small groups. If you have written about yourself or someone from your country, you can bring in pictures of your family and your native country.

 If you wrote your paragraph about yourself, or about one of the people in the picture on page 92, now interview a classmate. Write about his or her experiences. If you already wrote about someone else, write a paragraph about yourself.

Journal Writing

 Write in your journal for ten or fifteen minutes about one or both of the following topics.

1. Write for fifteen minutes on the feelings you had when you first arrived in North America. If you wish, exchange your work with a partner and compare your experiences.
2. Write for fifteen minutes on how you feel about life in your new country right now. If you wish, choose a partner and discuss the differences between your feelings when you first arrived and your feelings now.

CHAPTER eight

Tastes and Preferences

You are going to write a composition comparing two types of housing.

in this chapter

STEPS TO **writing**

1. Exploring Ideas

exercise 1

As a class or in small groups, look at the pictures below. Discuss the types of housing situations. How are they similar? How are they different? What kind(s) of housing do you prefer? What kind(s) don't you like? Why?

You are going to write a composition comparing two different types of housing. You will write about how they are similar and how they are different.

exercise 2

Work with a partner or in small groups. Find students who live in different kinds of housing. Take turns discussing your different housing situations. Describe the advantages and disadvantages of—and what you like and don't like about—your type of housing. Ask questions and take notes.

If the students in your class live in many different housing situations, work with another partner or group. Discuss your situations again, so that everyone can learn about all the different situations. When you finish discussing them, choose two different kinds of housing to write about.

WHAT DO YOU THINK?

Finding a Basis of Comparison

You are going to write a comparison for this chapter. When you compare situations, places, things, or people, there must be a basis of comparison. That is, even though the items may be very different, they must have something basic in common. For example, although a rock musician and the pope both may be famous people, being famous is not enough of a basis of comparison. You might, however, compare the pope as a leader of a church to the president of the United States as a leader of a country.

Practice this by looking at the following list. With a partner, decide if each pair has enough similarities to compare them successfully:

1. the Nile River / New York City
2. a police officer / a coal miner
3. a baby / an old man
4. Brasilia / your neighborhood
5. a tricycle / a pair of skis
6. bike riding / skiing
7. San Francisco / Tel Aviv
8. the Amazon River / the Mississippi River

exercise 3

Write about the two types of housing that you chose. Write as much as you can about them in ten minutes.

 **exercise 4**

As a class, discuss your notes from Exercise 3 about the two types of housing. What characteristics can you compare? Discuss the list of characteristics below. Did you think of these characteristics? Did you think of other characteristics? Add them to the list.

privacy
expense
personal space
public space
responsibilities
rights

social life
access to university facilities
access to stores, etc.
safety
comfort

Building Vocabulary

 **exercise 5**

Here are some words that you may be able to use in your comparisons. Did you use any others in the notes you wrote? If so, add them to the list.

ADJECTIVES	NOUNS	VERBS
accessible	roommate	share
inexpensive	housemate	divide
lonesome	companionship	concentrate
cozy	chores	prefer
spacious	rooming house	
self-sufficient	landlady	_____
dependable	landlord	_____
exorbitant	utilities	_____
convenient	rent	_____
cheap	public transportation	_____
tidy	solitude	_____
orderly		_____
messy	_____	_____
on-campus	_____	_____
off-campus	_____	_____
	_____	_____
_____	_____	_____
_____	_____	
_____		

 **exercise 6**

Look at the adjectives in the list in Exercise 5. How many opposites can you find? Can you think of any others?

2. Organizing Ideas
Listing Similarities and Differences

Look at this example of some possible similarities and differences between living at home and living with another family.

SIMILARITIES

Both: not lonely
    less stressful
    family support in an
      emergency

DIFFERENCES

at home
more comfortable and familiar
less expensive

with another family
little household responsibility
more privacy

Make a list of the similarities and differences between the living situations you chose.

SIMILARITIES

Both: _____

_____

_____

_____

_____

_____

_____

DIFFERENCES

Living situation A: _____

_____

_____

Living situation B: _____

_____

_____

_____

focus on testing

Listing Ideas for a Comparison

In Exercise 1, you practiced listing similarities and differences between living situations. It's particularly useful to list ideas like these when you have to write a comparison for a timed writing test. Before you start writing, take some scratch paper and jot down everything that comes to mind on the topic. You'll quickly see that you have a lot to say, maybe even too much. Group the similarities and the differences, and cross out anything that is unrelated or unimportant. Then use what you have left to write your essay.

 Look at the two lists. Decide whether there are more similarities or differences between the situations you chose. If there are more similarities, you will want to focus on the similarities in your composition, although you will also have to mention the differences. If there are more differences, you will have to focus on them.

 Read this composition comparing renting a room with a family and living with your own family. Does the composition focus more on similarities or differences?

FAMILY LIFE

Living at home and renting a room in another family's house are different living situations, but there are some important similarities. Living at home is less expensive of course, and it is more comfortable to live with people you know. On the other hand, you may not have much privacy at home, and you will probably have to do some household work. In contrast, renting a room in a family home is more expensive, but you have little household responsibility (although students are usually expected to do their own laundry). While you probably have more privacy living with another family, you may feel more awkward living with people that you don't know well.

There are several similarities between these two kinds of living arrangements. Students who live in a family situation don't often feel lonely. There are usually people around for you to interact with. Also, in a family situation, you have the convenience of home-cooked meals; you don't have to spend time shopping for and cooking food, and the food is probably better than fast food or food from the school cafeteria. Finally, if you get sick or some other emergency happens, the family can help you. Because of these important aspects, both of these situations are less stressful than other, more independent living arrangements.

Writing Topic Sentences

 Look at the first sentence of the preceding composition. It is the topic sentence of the whole composition and identifies the situations that the writer is comparing. Which part focuses on the similarities? Which part focuses on the differences?

 **exercise 5**   Tell whether the focus of the compositions with these topic sentences is on similarities or differences.

1. One of the most drastic changes that students going away to college face is the change from living at home with their families to living in a dorm with hundreds of other students.
2. If you don't mind sharing a room in a dormitory, then you will probably enjoy apartment living because there are many important similarities.

 **exercise 6**   Write a topic sentence for your paragraph. You can use structures similar to the ones just given.

Analyzing the Organization of a Composition

 **exercise 7**   Answer these questions about the organization of the composition "Family Living."

1. Which paragraph describes the similarities? Which one describes the differences? What is the topic sentence of the second paragraph?
2. Look at these vocabulary items. Which ones does the writer use to show similarities? Which ones show differences?

   both   while   on the other hand   more   less

3. What transitional expressions does the writer use when mentioning additional similarities and differences?
4. Does the writer use any comparative structures (more + adjective, adjective + -er)?

3. Developing Cohesion and Style

Using *Both* in Comparisons

> There are several different ways to use *both* in a sentence that shows similarities.
>
> 1. Before nouns:
>
>   *example:*   *Both* situations are safe and inexpensive.
>
> 2. As a pronoun:
>
>   *example:*   *Both* are safe and inexpensive.

3. With verbs (note the position of *both* with different types of verbs):

examples: They are *both* safe and inexpensive. (*Both* follows the verb *be.*)
They have *both* given me a lot. (*Both* follows the first auxiliary verb.)
They *both* offer convenience. (*Both* goes before one-word verbs except *be.*)

Using *Neither* in Comparisons

You can use *neither* to show negative similarities. Note that *neither* is always singular.

1. With *nor.*

   example: *Neither* living in a dorm *nor* sharing an apartment is ideal.

2. Before a singular noun.

   example: *Neither* situation is ideal.

3. As a pronoun

   example: *Neither* is ideal.

Rooming House Rules

- **No smoking**
- **No male/female visitors in bedroom**
- **Wash all dishes after you eat**
- **No loud music after 10 pm**
- **Turn off television when you leave**
- **Ask permission before receiving overnight guests**

Dormitory Rules

- **No smoking**
- **No male/female visitors after 10 pm**
- **Please keep kitchen clean**
- **No loud music**
- **Turn off television when you leave**
- **Permission required for overnight guests**

**exercise 1** Write sentences about the rules and facilities at the rooming house and the dormitory. The first one is done as an example.

1. allow / smoking <u>Neither place allows smoking.</u>

_____

2. have / kitchen _____

_____

3. play / loud music _____

_____

4. television / available _____

_____

5. allow / male visitors _____

_____

6. require permission / overnight guests _____

_____

**exercise 2** Write two sentences about the similarities of the situations you chose. Use neither or both.

_____

_____

Using While to Show Contrast

You can use while to show two different or opposite ideas in a sentence. Note that you can use while before either clause of the sentence and that a comma is used in both sentences.

examples: While living at home is inexpensive, sharing an apartment can cost a lot of money.
Living at home is inexpensive, while sharing an apartment can cost a lot of money.

exercise 3 Look at these lists showing the differences between living on campus and living off campus. Write two sentences with *while* to show the differences as in the example.

ON CAMPUS	OFF CAMPUS
-makes it easy to get to classes	-may require a long commute
-you feel separated from the community	-you feel part of the community
-must share a room	-it's possible to have a room to yourself
-you feel a part of campus life	-you may feel separated from campus life
-must eat cafeteria food	-you can cook your own food

Living on campus makes it easy to get to classes, while living
off campus may require a long commute.

While living on campus makes it easy to get to classes, living off
campus may require a long commute.

_____

_____

_____

_____

_____

_____

Using Expressions of Contrast:
In Contrast and *On the Other Hand*

The expressions *in contrast* and *on the other hand* have similar meanings. You can use them to present information that is different from or the opposite of some previous information.

examples	notes
Renting an apartment can be expensive. *In contrast,* living at home is inexpensive. Living at home is inexpensive. Renting an apartment, *in contrast,* is more expensive.	*In contrast* is used to contrast two different or opposite things. For variety, you can use *in contrast* after the subject; if you do, use two commas.
An apartment gives you more privacy. *On the other hand,* dorm life is a lot of fun. Renting a room is more expensive. *On the other hand,* you have little household responsibility.	*On the other hand* is often used to contrast advantages and disadvantages of the same thing (for example, renting a room).

exercise  In the following sentences, insert *in addition* to show additional similar information. Insert *in contrast* or *on the other hand* to show contrasting information.

1. Living in a dorm means that you are always surrounded by people. Apartment life can be quite lonely.

2. A rooming house is a good solution for those who like small groups of people. There's almost always someone to talk to.

3. In an apartment, you can usually cook your own meals. In a dorm you usually have to eat cafeteria food.

4. Living in a dorm is an exciting new experience. Staying at home with your family is just like being in high school.

4. Writing the First Draft

Write your composition using the organization you came up with at the beginning of this chapter. Use both and neither to show similarities. Use while, in contrast, on the other hand to show differences. You can also use however and although to show contrast. Write on every other line so that you can revise your paragraph easily.

5. Editing Practice

Using Gerunds

A gerund is the -ing form of a verb used as a noun. It can be used as a subject or an object. Gerunds are used as uncountable nouns.

- As the subject of a verb in general statements:

  example: Living in a dorm is fun.
  Doing housework and paying bills are part of apartment life.

- As the object of a verb:

  example: I like living in a dorm.

- As the subject or object after the:

  example: Who does the cooking in your house?

- As the complement of a sentence:

  example: Two of the disadvantages of apartment life are doing housework and paying bills.

- As the object of a preposition:

  example: You should try living on campus before deciding to live off campus.

 **exercise 1**   Complete each sentence with the gerund form of a verb or verb phrase from the list below.

live	do chores	be independent	shop
cook	pay bills	rent an apartment	have

1. _____ and _____ for yourself can take a lot of time.

2. _____ is the best part of apartment living.

3. _____ no privacy is a big disadvantage of dormitory life.

4. _____ is only for mature responsible students.

5. _____ at home with your family gives you a lot of security.

 Write two sentences with gerunds for your paragraph.

_____

_____

Using Comparatives and Superlatives

Comparatives

To compare two people or things, use the pattern adjective + *-er* (+ *than*) or *more/less* + adjective (+ *than*).

examples	notes
A rooming house is *cheaper than* a dorm. (A rooming house is *cheaper*.)	One-syllable adjectives usually take the *-er* (+ *than*) ending.
Dorms are *noisier than* apartments. (Dorms are *noisier*.)	Two-syllable adjectives can take either the *-er* (+ *than*) ending or the words *more* or *less* (+ *than*).
An apartment is *more expensive than* a dorm. (An apartment is more *expensive*.)	Adjectives with more than two syllables always take *more* or *less* (+ *than*).
Paul is *happier than* Jack is about living in a dorm.	With two-syllable adjectives that end in *-y*, change the *y* to *i* before adding *-er*.
Apartments are *better than* dorms. Living in a dorm is *worse than* living at home.	Some irregular comparatives include: *good-better; bad-worse; far-farther/further.*

Superlatives

To describe something that has the greatest or least amount of a quality compared to two or more other things, use the pattern *the* + adjective + *-est* or *the* + *most/least* + adjective.

examples	**notes**
Living at home is *the cheapest* accomodation you can find. For many students, apartment life is probably *the most difficult.* A dorm offers *the least privacy.*	One-syllable adjectives usually take the *-est* ending. Most adjectives with more than one syllable take *most/least.*
Living in an apartment is *the best situation* for independent people. Living at home is *the worst choice* if you want to be independent.	Irregular superlatives include: *the best; the worst; the farthest/furthest.*

 Write the sentences using the comparative or superlative forms of the adjectives in parentheses.

1. A rooming house is _____ (economical) than an apartment.

2. Of all the possibilities, students probably feel _____ (free) in an apartment.

3. Even though there are campus police, it's hard to say that living on campus is _____ (safe) than living off.

4. My room is small but it's _____ (cozy) than my room in the dorm.

5. For many people, dorm life is the _____ (stressful).

 Edit this paragraph for errors in the use of comparatives and superlatives.

The decision to live on or off campus is a very important one. It may affect your whole college career. Both situations have advantages and disadvantages and which one you choose depends a lot on what is important to you. For example, on-campus housing is generally much convenienter than off-campus housing. It's more easy to get to class, especially early in the morning. Students who live on campus are also more closer to facilities such as the library and gym. On the other hand, in a dorm, you usually have to share a room, while off-campus housing can be much more private and least noisy. Cafeteria food is another disadvantage of on-campus housing. Students on special diets will often find it difficult to live in a dormitory than to live in a rooming house or apartment, where they can cook for themselves.

6. Editing Your Writing

Edit your composition using the checklist below. First, check your paragraph for content, organization, cohesion and style using items 1, 2, and 3 in the checklist. Then edit your paragraph for grammar and form using items 4 and 5.

Editing Checklist

1. Content
   Does your composition list all the similarities and differences you think are important?
2. Organization
   a. Does the topic sentence mention both similarities and differences even though it focuses on one or the other?
   b. Does one paragraph deal with differences and the other with similarities?
3. Cohesion and Style
   Have you used such expressions as *both, neither, in contrast, on the other hand*, and *while*?
4. Grammar
   a. Have you used gerunds correctly?
   b. Have you used comparatives and superlatives correctly?
5. Form
   a. Have you used a capital letter to begin each sentence?
   b. Have you used a period to end each sentence?

Exchange papers with another student and edit each other's compositions. Discuss any questions you have with your partner.

7. Writing the Second Draft

Rewrite your composition neatly, using good handwriting and correct form. Then give it to your teacher for comments.

A STEP **beyond**

activity 1   Find a comparison for two things or two people in a newspaper or magazine. Note the words and expressions the writer uses in the comparison. Is he or she focusing mainly on differences or similarities?

activity 2   Write a paragraph comparing two classes that you have had. They may be about the same subject or different subjects. When you finish, give your paragraph to a partner to read.

Journal Writing

activity 3   Write in your journal for 15 minutes about one or both of the following topics.

1. Write about the similarities and differences between your high school and your college.
2. Write a comparison of two things or two people. You may choose types of music, cities, kinds of transportation, politicians, anything that has basis for comparison.

CHAPTER nine

Discoveries

You are going to write a description of a planet.

STEPS TO writing

1. Exploring Ideas

Obtaining Information from Pictures, Charts, and Tables

Students often have to use pictures, charts, and tables to get accurate information that they need to write about certain subjects. This is especially true in the physical and social sciences. In this chapter, you will practice getting information from these sources.

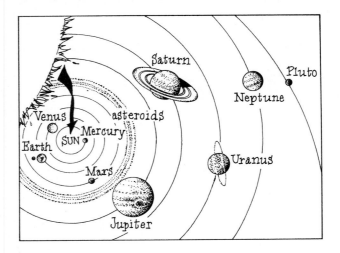

exercise 1 Look at the picture above and the charts and tables on pages 125–127. Answer the following questions.

1. Which planet is the largest?
2. Which planet is the farthest from the sun?
3. Which planet has the most moons?
4. Which planet rotates the most slowly?
5. Which planet has the fastest rotation?
6. How many moons does Saturn have?
7. When was Uranus discovered?
8. Which planets have been visited by spacecraft?
9. What is Mars' atmosphere made of?
10. What is an interesting feature of Jupiter?
11. Who discovered Pluto?
12. What is Venus also called?
13. Which planets have rings?

	average temperature	diameter (in miles)	number of moons
Mercury	950°F on sunny side; −350°F on dark side	3,032	0
Venus	800°F	7,523	0
Earth	59°F	7,928	1
Mars	extremes are 65°F to −190°F	4,218	2
Jupiter	19,300°F	88,900	16
Saturn	−228°F in atmosphere	74,900	23
Uranus	−270°F	31,800	15
Neptune	−330°F	30,800	8
Pluto	no information	1,400	1

	rotation	distance from sun (millions of miles)	revolution around sun
Mercury	58.6 days	36	88 days
Venus	243 days	67.2	224.7 days
Earth	23:56 hrs./mins.	92.9	365.26 days
Mars	24:37 hrs./mins.	141.5	687 days
Jupiter	9:55 hrs./mins.	483.4	11.9 years
Saturn	10:39 hrs./mins.	884.6	29.5 years
Uranus	17 hrs.	1783.8	84 years
Neptune	17.7 hrs.	2793.9	164.79 years
Pluto	6.39 days	3690.5	247.7 years

Jupiter

	composition of atmosphere	features
Mercury	little or no atmosphere	craters like the moon
Venus	carbon dioxide	220-m.p.h. winds
Earth	nitrogen, oxygen	
Mars	carbon dioxide, nitrogen, argon, oxygen	bright red color; polar ice caps; volcanoes
Jupiter	hydrogen, helium, water, ammonia, methane	Great Red Spot, 25,000 miles long; several rings
Saturn	hydrogen, helium	huge system of rings of rock and ice
Uranus	hydrogen, helium, methane	10 rings and 15 moons; ocean of superheated water
Neptune	hydrogen, helium, methane	cloudy, fluid atmosphere, and rocky core
Pluto	no information	consists mainly of water ice with a crust of methane ice

	planet discovery	exploration and new discoveries
Mercury		in 1975 Mariner 10 found magnetic field, which surprised scientists
Venus		Soviet Spacecraft Venera 8 landed on Venus in 1972, sent information for one hour, was then destroyed by heat
Mars		Viking spacecraft landed in 1975, analyzed soil samples
Jupiter		Pioneers 10 and 11 sent back photographs in 1975; Voyagers 1 and 2 sent back moving pictures in 1979
Saturn		Pioneer 11, 1979
Uranus	Sir William Herschel, 1781	Voyager 2 sent back pictures in 1986; discovered 10 new moons and a strong magnetic field
Neptune	Gottfried Galle, 1846	Voyager 2 flew by in 1989; discovered 3 rings and 6 new moons
Pluto	C. W. Tombaugh, 1930	

Venus	also known as the Morning Star or Evening Star; rotates from west to east
Mercury	no atmosphere
Mars	changes color; scientists believe it has seasons
Jupiter	Great Red Spot (cloud system); composition like the sun's
Saturn	huge cloud system, mostly white ammonia clouds
Uranus	greenish glow
Neptune	bluish color; partial rings (arcs) that do not completely circle the planet; discovered because astronomers wanted to know why Uranus sometimes speeded up and at other times slowed down
Pluto	irregular orbit; is sometimes the eighth planet, but normally the ninth planet, from the sun

 **exercise 2**   In this chapter you are going to write a paragraph describing a planet. Select a planet other than Earth or Uranus. Study the information about the planet given on the preceding pages and complete this chart with the correct information. You may not be able to find information for every category for each planet.

Name: _____

Size: _____

Distance from the sun: _____

Composition: _____

Rotation: _____

Revolution around the sun: _____

Discovered: _____

Exploration / New discoveries: _____

Moons: _____

Interesting features: _____

_____

Other information:

_____

_____

WHAT DO YOU THINK?

Speculating

When you speculate about a subject, you make guesses based on what you already know about it. Speculating is useful when discussing or writing about scientific subjects.

Practice this skill by speculating about the planet you have chosen. First, answer these questions:

- **Can the planet you have chosen to write about support life? Why or why not?**

  _____

  _____

- **What information from the chart helped you decide?**

  _____

  _____

Now, share your answers with a partner.

Saturn

Building Vocabulary

 **exercise 3**

In filling out the preceding chart, you may have found that you don't know the English words for some of the concepts you want to express. Find the words you need and add them to the list below.

NOUNS	VERBS	ADJECTIVES
atmosphere	be composed of	inhabited
composition	discover	uninhabited
diameter	explore	rocky
discover	inhabit	_____
discovery	revolve	_____
exploration	rotate	_____
orbit	_____	_____
revolution	_____	_____
rotation		
_____	_____	_____
_____	_____	_____
_____	_____	_____
_____	_____	_____
_____	_____	_____

exercise 4

In writing about a planet, you will probably need to use expressions to describe the planet's position, movements, and composition. What other expressions can you think of? Add them to the list.

LOCATION/MOTION	COMPOSITION
is surrounded by	is composed of
lies between	is made of
passes by / passes close to	was formed by
revolves around	_____
rotates	
_____	_____
_____	_____

examples: The atmosphere of Saturn is composed of hydrogen and helium.
Two moons revolve around Mars.

2. Organizing Ideas
Making Comparisons

> One way to make your paragraph more interesting is to tell the reader how the planet you are writing about is different from the earth or the other planets.

 Look at your notes. Compare the planet you chose to Earth. Answer these questions.

1. Is it very much larger or smaller?
2. Does it have a much longer or shorter period of rotation / revolution?
3. Is it much hotter or colder?
4. Is it much farther from the sun?

 Think of some other ways to compare Earth and the planet you chose.

_____

_____

_____

_____

exercise 3 Compare the planet you chose to the other planets. Answer these questions.

1. Is it the largest or one of the largest? The smallest or one of the smallest?
2. Is its atmosphere very different from the others?
3. Do scientists know a lot more or less about it than they do about other planets?

exercise 4

Finally, think of some other ways to compare your planet to the others in the solar system. Make notes of any interesting comparisons you have found. Remember, the greater the difference, the more interesting your comparison will be.

_____

_____

_____

_____

focus on testing

Making Comparisons Interesting

Exercises 1 and 3 ask you to answer questions about the notes you made on your planet. Asking yourself questions like these will help you make your writing more interesting when you have to write a comparison for a timed test. Before you start writing in a testing situation, think of as many ways to compare your subjects as possible. Ask yourself questions—like the ones on page 130—that help you explore these areas. Jot down your answers and use them in your essay.

Ordering Information in a Paragraph

In writing about your planet, you do not have to present information in any particular order. However, it is important to keep related information together.

exercise 5

These six topics describe the information given in the paragraph on the next page. The topics are not in the correct order. Read the paragraph. Then number the topics according to the order in which they are presented in the paragraph. The first one is done for you.

_____ Exploration

_____ Discovery

_____ Length of year, day

_____ Composition of atmosphere

__1__ Position

_____ Features

Uranus, the seventh planet in the solar system, lies between the planets of Saturn and Neptune. Uranus's orbit is much larger than Earth's. It takes this planet 84 Earth-years to complete its trip around the sun. However, a day on Uranus is shorter than a day on Earth. It lasts only 17 hours. Uranus was discovered in 1781 by the British astronomer Sir William Herschel. In 1986, the Voyager 2 spaceship passed by Uranus and took pictures. Before this exploration, not much was known about the planet. Scientific studies have now shown that its atmosphere is composed of hydrogen, helium, and methane and has a temperature of approximately −270°F. The planet has deep oceans of very hot water and a bright glow. The Voyager 2 pictures also showed that Uranus has ten rings and fifteen moons. Scientists hope to learn much more about this distant planet in the future.

 **exercise 6**   Look at the notes for your paragraph and put them in the order you wish to state them.

3. Developing Cohesion and Style

Using the Passive Voice

The passive voice is used in both spoken and written English. It is often used in scientific or technical writing. In sentences in the active voice, the main focus is on the subject (the agent or doer of the action). In the passive voice, the main focus is on the object (the person or thing acted upon). Compare:

Active Voice: Nine planets *orbit* the sun.   *Main focus* = nine planets

Passive Voice: The sun *is orbited by* nine planets.   *Main focus* = the sun

All passive voice sentences contain a form of *be* + the past participle of the main verb. *By* + agent noun can be used in a passive voice sentence to tell who or what performed the action of a verb. *By* + agent is used in a passive sentence with new or important information; if the information is not important, it can be omitted.

	examples	notes
Active	Sir William Herschel *discovered* Uranus.	The subject *Sir William Herschel* is important; it cannot be omitted from this passive sentence.
Passive	Uranus *was discovered by* Sir William Herschel.	
Active	People *make* telescopes with a series of lenses.	The subject *people* is obvious. It is not important to the sentence. It can be omitted from the passive sentence.
Passive	Telescopes *are made* by people with a series of lenses	

Note: The verbs below are often used in the passive voice, but they usually do not use *by*. Instead, other prepositions follow these verbs.

The moon is not *composed of* green cheese.
　　　　　　　 made (up) of

She is *known for* her scientific discoveries.
　　　 noted for

Satellites *are used to* explore space.
　　　　　　 used for exploring space.

A view of the moon

exercise **1** Complete the following paragraph with the appropriate passive or active forms of the verbs in parentheses. Don't forget to put the verb in the correct tense.

THE MOON

　　　　The moon ＿＿＿＿＿＿＿ (orbit) the Earth the way the earth ＿＿＿＿＿＿＿
　　　　　　　　　　　　　　　 1　　　　　　　　　　　　　　　　　　　　　　2

(orbit) the sun. Scientists believe that the moon ＿＿＿＿＿＿＿ (form) at about
　　　　　　　　　　　　　　　　　　　　　　　　　　　　　 3

the same time as the earth. They now know that it ＿＿＿＿＿＿＿ (make up of)
　　　　　　　　　　　　　　　　　　　　　　　　　　　　　　 4

many of the same materials. But scientists ＿＿＿＿＿＿＿ (find) that the moon
　　　　　　　　　　　　　　　　　　　　　　　　　 5

is different from the earth in many ways. For example, the moon

＿＿＿＿＿＿＿ (have) no atmosphere to carry sound; as a result, no matter
　　 6

what ＿＿＿＿＿＿＿ (happen) on the moon's surface, no sound ＿＿＿＿＿＿＿
　　　　　　 7　　　　　　　　　　　　　　　　　　　　　　　　　　　　　　 8

(hear). Without an atmosphere, water _____ (disappear) into space.

That is why no water can _____ (find) on the surface of the moon,
₉
₁₀

although some water _____ (trap) inside rocks. Without water, there
₁₁

can _____ (be) no weather. So if you go to the moon, you will never
₁₂

_____ (see) a cloud, _____ (get) wet in a rainstorm, or
₁₃ ₁₄

_____ (feel) the wind blow.
₁₅

 **exercise 2**

Look at the notes you made for your paragraph. Write three sentences in the passive voice about your planet based on your notes. Show your sentences to a classmate. Can he or she find any errors?

Varying Word Order: *With* + Noun Phrase

You can make your paragraph more interesting by changing the order of the elements in your sentence. For example, you can occasionally begin a sentence with a clause using with + noun phrase.

When you use this type of clause, you must make sure that the noun modified by the clause comes directly <u>after</u> the clause. Compare:

Incorrect: With a temperature of 800°F, <u>no life</u> could survive on Venus.

Correct: With a temperature of 800°F, <u>Venus</u> is much too hot for life to survive.

The second sentence is correct because <u>Venus</u> (not <u>no life</u>) has a temperature of 800°F.

 **exercise 3**

Match the clauses in Column A with the clauses in Column B. Use the charts and tables on pages 125–127 if necessary.

A

1. _____ With its beautiful rings,

2. _d_ With a diameter of only 3,032 miles,

3. _____ With a daytime temperature of 800°F,

4. _____ With its bright red color and changing surface features,

B

a. Mars has interested astronomers for a long time.

b. Venus could not support life.

c. Saturn is the most spectacular planet in the solar system.

d. Pluto is the smallest planet in the solar system.

exercise 4   Write a sentence about your planet using *with* + noun phrase.

_____

_____

Using *Unlike* + Noun Phrase to Show Contrast

> Another way to make your paragraph more interesting is to begin a sentence by contrasting the planet you are writing about to Earth or to the other planets.
>
> _examples:_   *Unlike all the other planets,* Venus rotates from west to east.
> *Unlike Earth,* Mercury has no atmosphere.

exercise 5   Complete each of the following sentences.

1. Unlike Earth, Mars

_____

2. Unlike Uranus and Neptune, Pluto

_____

3. Unlike Earth, Jupiter

_____

4. Unlike the other planets, Mercury

_____

Giving Reasons with *Because of* + Noun Phrase and *Because* + Clause

> You have already learned how to use *because* to connect two clauses.
>
> _example:_   No one can live on Mercury *because* it is very hot.
>
> The phrase *because of* is used with a noun phrase rather than a clause.
>
> _example:_   No one can live on Mercury *because of* its high temperature.
>
> Note that *because* is followed by a subject and a verb, but *because of* is followed by a noun.

Both *because* and *because of* can be used in the middle or at the beginning of a sentence. When you begin a sentence with *because* or *because of,* you must remember to put a comma after the first clause or phrase.

examples: Pluto is sometimes the eighth planet in the solar system *because* it has an irregular orbit.
Because it has an irregular orbit, Pluto is sometimes the eighth planet in the solar system.
Pluto is sometimes the eighth planet in the solar system *because of* its irregular orbit.
Because of its irregular orbit, Pluto is sometimes the eighth planet in the solar system.

 **exercise 6** Add *because of* or *because* to the phrases and clauses in Column A. Then match the terms in Column A and Column B to make logical sentences. The first one is done as an example.

A

1. Because of _____ its irregular orbit,

2. _____ its distance from the sun,

3. _____ a desire to learn more about the solar system,

4. _____ our need for oxygen,

5. _____ it is close to Earth,

6. _____ its orbit is much larger than Earth's,

7. _____ pictures taken by Voyager 2,

B

a. Uranus takes 84 Earth-years to travel around the sun.

b. scientists learned that Uranus has eleven rings and fifteen moons.

c. Pluto is extremely cold.

d. Pluto is sometimes the eighth planet in the solar system.

e. many spaceships have been launched.

f. Mars has always interested skywatchers.

g. human beings could not live on Mars.

 **exercise 7** Write a sentence about your planet using *because* or *because of.*

_____

_____

4. Writing the First Draft

Write your paragraph using the chart you filled out in Exercise 2 in Exploring Ideas. Use the passive voice when necessary. Try to compare your planet with Earth or the other planets. Make your paragraph more interesting by varying the sentence structure with *unlike* + noun phrase and *with* + noun phrase. Give reasons with *because* or *because of*. Write on every other line so you can revise your paragraph easily.

5. Editing Practice
Using the Passive Voice

 Edit this paragraph for errors in the use of the passive voice, and rewrite it correctly.

URANUS

Uranus, the seventh planet in the solar system, locates between the planets of Saturn and Neptune. Uranus's orbit is much larger than Earth's.

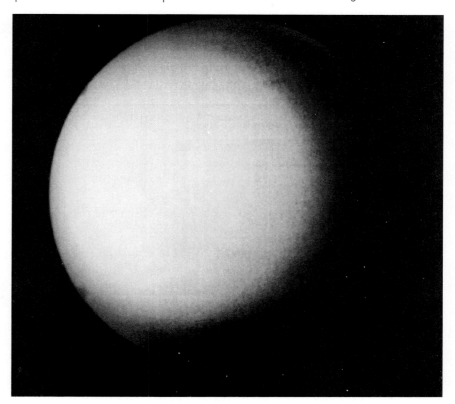

This planet's trip around the sun is taked in 84 Earth-years. However, a day on Uranus is shorter than a day on Earth. It lasts only 17 hours. Uranus be discovered in 1781 by the British astronomer Sir William Herschel. In 1986 the Voyager 2 spaceship was passed by Uranus and took pictures; before that, not much had learned about its composition. Scientific studies have now been shown that its atmosphere is composing of hydrogen, helium, and methane and has a temperature of approximately −270°F. It has deep oceans of very hot water and a bright glow. The Voyager 2 pictures also show that Uranus has eleven rings and fifteen moons. Scientists hope to learn much more about this distant planet in the future.

6. Editing Your Writing

Edit your composition using the checklist below. First, check your paragraph for content, organization, cohesion and style using items 1, 2, and 3 in the checklist. Then edit your paragraph for grammar and form using items 4 and 5.

Editing Checklist

1. Content
   a. Is your information accurate?
   b. Have you made interesting comparisons?
2. Organization
   Is the information organized logically?
3. Cohesion and Style
   a. Did you vary the word order in some sentences, using *with* + noun phrase, *because* and *because of*?
   b. Did you use *unlike* + noun phrase to show contrast?
4. Grammar
   a. Did you use the passive voice correctly?
   b. Did you use correct tenses?
5. Form
   a. Did you use correct paragraph format? (indentation, division of words between syllables, margins)
   b. Did you use correct punctuation? (capitalization, commas, periods)
   c. Did you check the spelling of the words you are not sure of?

 **exercise 2** Exchange papers with another classmate and edit each other's paragraphs. Circle or underline in pencil any words, phrases, or sentences that you don't understand or that you think need to be corrected. Then return your paragraphs. Discuss any questions you have with your partner.

7. Writing the Second Draft

> After you edit your paragraph, rewrite it neatly, using good handwriting and correct form. Then give your composition to your teacher for comments.

A STEP **beyond**

 **activity 1** Find a description of how an object (for example, a tool or an appliance) is used. Appliance or user's manuals (written material that comes with the product when you buy it) are good sources of this kind of writing. Note the use of the passive voice. Is it used a lot? A little? Are the instructions generally clear? Why or why not?

 **activity 2** Imagine that your classmate is from another planet and has never seen an object that you use every day—for example, a telephone or a pencil. Write a paragraph describing it to him or her. Then exchange paragraphs.

 **activity 3** In small groups, talk about some new discoveries and inventions you think will be made in the next twenty years. These might be discoveries or inventions in technology (e.g., new machines), medicine (e.g., new types of surgery or cures for diseases), astronomy (e.g., new information about planets), etc. Make a list of your discoveries and inventions. In which countries do you think each of them will be made? Write the names of the counties next to the items on your list. When you finish your list, choose one discovery or invention that you believe will be most important. Put a check (√) next to it.

Join another group of students and compare your lists. How are they similar? How are they different? Is there agreement about where you think the discoveries or inventions will be made? About which discovery or invention will be most important? What are some reasons for your choices?

Journal Writing

 **activity 4**

Write for fifteen minutes about one or more of the following topics.

1. Write a paragraph describing a full moon to a blind person. Hint: Think about how the things you *see* would *feel* if you could touch them.
2. Write about the following topic: Would you like to travel in space? Why or why not?
3. Write about what you believe will be the most important discovery or invention in the next twenty years. Who do you think will make it? Why will it be so important? Who will benefit? How will they benefit?

CHAPTER ten

Medicine, Myths, and Magic

in this chapter

You are going to write an argumentative composition about this issue: "Some children are born with severe mental handicaps. Should parents and doctors of these children be allowed to let them die?"

STEPS TO **writing**

1. Exploring Ideas
Discussing Medical Issues

exercise **1**   Look at the pictures and discuss these questions.

1. What do you know about the handicaps that these children have? What other kinds of handicaps do you know about?
2. Do you know about any treatments or special programs for handicapped children?
3. How are children with handicaps treated in your home country? Where would someone who has a handicapped child go for help? What kinds of help are available?
4. Do you know any superstitious beliefs (beliefs that are not based on scientific fact) about possible causes of handicaps? Why do you think some people might have such beliefs?
5. Do you know anyone who has a serious handicap? How does she or he deal with it?

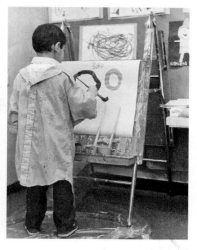

Some children are born with severe brain damage. Many live their lives with a mental age lower than one year.

Although some people with cerebral palsy are mentally retarded, many have normal intelligence. They have problems with muscle control and may also be blind or deaf.

exercise **2**

Read these accounts by parents of children with severe mental handicaps. Then, in small groups, discuss the questions.

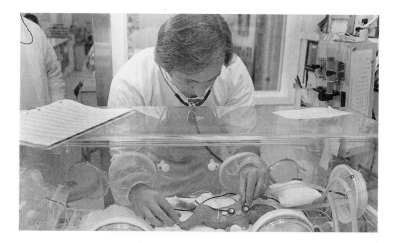

Baby in an intensive-care nursery

My daughter Tracy was born prematurely. A few days after her birth, a blood hemorrhage (a heavy flow of blood) destroyed part of her brain. The doctors said that she would be severely mentally retarded and would probably not walk or talk. With the help of our doctor, we decided that if her heart should fail, the doctors should not try to bring her back to life. But the hospital said this was not our decision to make, because the law requires them to keep all babies alive, even if their brains are severely damaged.

So Tracy stayed in the hospital for six months, at a cost of $300,000. She was on different machines and had several operations. It became difficult for me to visit her in the hospital without feeling sick because it seemed to me that they were torturing her. Now she is home with us. We love her very much, but she is not developing mentally and we feel that she will not be able to lead a real life. We still feel it would have been better to let her die a natural death instead of keeping her alive artifically.

. . .

My son Grant is four years old. A few days after he was born, he developed a severe brain infection. The doctors treated him with antibiotics, but after a week the infection had damaged a great deal of his brain. Several doctors examined him and said the damage was so great that he would probably be very retarded and that he could also develop cerebral palsy, blindness, and deafness. They suggested that we stop giving him the antibiotics and allow him to die. My husband and I could not do this—it seemed like murder to us.

After a few weeks, the infection was controlled and we were able to take him home from the hospital. He is in a wheelchair and will probably never walk or talk, but we can't make a judgment on his life. He smiles sometimes and gets upset sometimes. He doesn't live like most people, but I don't think he would want to die. I think that many doctors and parents aren't thinking of the child when they say we shouldn't treat brain-damaged children. They are thinking only of their problems.

1. How do the accounts you read affect how you feel about the problem?
2. What else do you know about this problem?

WHAT DO YOU THINK?

Distinguishing Provable Statements

When preparing to write about a controversial subject, it's important to be able to tell the difference between statements that are *provable* and statements that are *unprovable*. For example, look at the following statements:

- Children with Down's syndrome have moderate to severe mental retardation.
- Children with Down's syndrome should not be allowed to go to school with normal children.

The first statement is provable; it's the result of scientific study, and you can find support for it in scientific material on Down's syndrome. The second statement cannot be proved; it's someone's opinion.

Practice this skill by studying the following statements. Work with a partner. Decide if each statement is provable or unprovable. If it's provable, write "P" next to it; if it's unprovable, write "U" next to it. Be prepared to explain your answers.

_____ Children born with severe mental retardation should not be kept alive.

_____ Most children with Down's syndrome do not live past the age of 35.

_____ Down's syndrome is a genetic disorder.

_____ A doctor who takes a patient off a life-support system is a murderer.

_____ Chinese medicine has a lot to offer Western medicine.

Building Vocabulary

 exercise 3 Add vocabulary from your discussion to this chart.

NOUNS	ADJECTIVES
blindness	blind
brain damage	brain-damaged
deafness	deaf
handicap	handicapped
mental retardation	mentally retarded
_____	_____
_____	_____
_____	_____
_____	_____

exercise 4 Adverbs of degree can modify adjectives; for example, *slightly retarded*. What are the adverb forms of these adjectives of degree?

ADJECTIVES	ADVERBS
moderate	_____
severe	_____
slight	_____

2. Organizing Ideas
Focusing on a Topic

You are going to write a three-point argumentative composition. In this essay, you will give three reasons to support your opinion. This composition will be at least five paragraphs long. It should be organized like this:

PARAGRAPH 1: Introduction: State your opinion on the topic.
PARAGRAPH 2: Develop the first reason for your opinion with a detailed example.
PARAGRAPH 3: Develop the second reason for your opinion with a detailed example.
PARAGRAPH 4: Develop the third reason for your opinion with a detailed example.
PARAGRAPH 5: Conclusion: Write a summary of your point of view.

In this kind of writing, it is important to choose a specific topic and focus on it clearly.

exercise 1

Read these introductions to an argumentative composition on the topic, "Should the families of dying people be allowed to take them off life-support machines and let them die?" How is the focus of each composition different? Discuss your answers in small groups.

1. People who have no hope of recovery and are kept alive only because of machines are not really living. Therefore, their families should be allowed to take them off life-support machines.

2. Doctors have the responsibility to keep people alive. A doctor who takes a patient off a life-support system is really murdering the person.

3. Because each situation is different, the family and doctors of a patient on a life-support system should decide whether or not to remove the person from the machines.

4. While many sick people in the world are dying because they don't have the money for proper medical care, we spend millions of dollars to keep people with no hope of recovery on life-support machines. We should use this money to help the people with a chance of recovery.

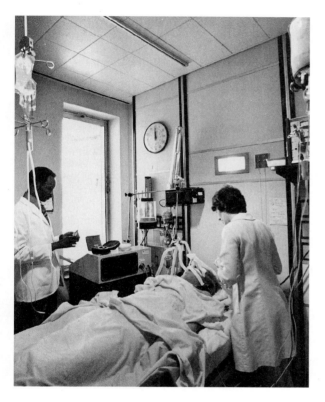

Patient on life-support machines

exercise 2

Write the introduction for your composition. State your opinion clearly and focus it on one particular idea.

_____

_____

_____

_____

_____

Supporting an Argument with Examples

> Good writers support their opinions with examples. You can use examples from your own experience or from articles you have read.

 What example is given in this composition? Underline it.

THE RIGHT TO CHOOSE

People on life-support machines are all different and in different situations. For that and other reasons, I believe the family and doctor of the patient on a life-support machine should be able to decide whether to remove the person from the machine or not. If the person on the machine is able to participate in the decision, he or she should definitely have the right to choose.

With modern technology, it is very difficult to determine what is real life and what is artificial life. Is a person who is breathing with the help of a machine but whose brain is dead really alive or not? No one can say for sure because each individual situation is different.

I recently saw a program on TV that illustrates how the government's interference causes great suffering. A machine was breathing for a man who was dying of cancer and he wanted to be removed from it. He said, "I want to live, but not tied to a machine." When he tried to turn off the machine himself, the doctors tied his hands to the bed because they thought the government would sue them if the man died. I think it is wrong to ignore the patient's wishes.

If a patient is still breathing with the help of machines but has no hope of recovery, the family of the patient may suffer greatly. Not only do they have problems mentally and psychologically because of the stress of such a situation, but they may be forced to spend huge amounts of money on these expensive machines. The same amount of money could save lives of people in other situations. The family may be financially ruined and still the patient has no hope.

I am against the use of life-support systems against the will of a patient, and his or her family and doctor. We live in a country where people have individual rights. One of these rights is the right to die with dignity.

Think of examples you can use to support your argument. You can use examples from your own experience or from one of the accounts given earlier in this chapter. Write your examples on the lines below.

_____

_____

_____

_____

_____

3. Developing Cohesion and Style

Using Restrictive Relative Clauses

> Restrictive relative clauses are often used to identify people, places, and things in writing. Commas are not used with restrictive clauses.
>
> examples: A machine was breathing for a man who was dying of cancer.
> We live in a country where people have individual rights.
> A machine that breathed for her was keeping her alive.

exercise 1   Complete these sentences with restrictive relative clauses beginning with who, that, or where.

1. I know a man _____

2. A hospital is a place _____

3. I saw a program on TV _____

_____

4. There are children _____

5. The child had a doctor _____

6. There are special machines _____

_____

Using Transitions and Giving Examples

The example from the composition "The Right to Choose" was introduced with this sentence:

> I recently saw a program on TV that illustrates how the government's interference causes great suffering.

That sentence is a transition sentence. It shows the purpose of the example. When you give an example, you can introduce it with expressions such as these:

_____ is a story/program/person that illustrates _____.

An example of _____ is _____.

_____ is an example of _____.

_____ shows _____.

I once knew _____.

exercise 2 Match these sentence parts to make transition sentences. Write the letter of the correct examples in the blanks after 1–4 below.

1. _____ The way in which my grandmother approached her death

2. _____ I once knew a handicapped person

3. _____ The story of my neighbor's children

4. _____ This story of a friend of my mother's shows

a. is an example of how the government can protect the rights of a handicapped child.

b. how difficult it is to raise a brain-damaged child.

c. who the doctors said would never walk or talk; but, he did.

d. showed that people can live with great pain and still die with dignity.

exercise 3 Write a transition sentence to introduce the example you are using.

_____

_____

_____

_____

_____

Using Quotations

Quotations can be used to support an argument in a composition. Both *direct quotations,* where you give the exact words of the speaker, and *indirect quotations,* where you give the general ideas of the speaker, can be used. (See the appendix for the rules on punctuation of direct quotations.)

examples: Direct quotation: He said, "I want to live, but not tied to a machine."
Indirect quotation: He said (that) he wanted to live,but not tied to a machine.

Remember to use the correct form of the verb in past-tense indirect quotations.

 **exercise 4**   Is there a direct or indirect quotation you can use in your composition? Write it here.

_____

_____

focus on testing

Using Quotations

In the box above, you read about using direct and indirect quotations in your writing. It's often difficult to use quotes in a testing situation, but if you *do,* your essay will make a powerful impression. Here's one way to use direct or indirect quotations on a test: Read a lot about the topic you think you will be tested on, and memorize a few statements beforehand.

Making Generalizations

Generalizations made in English are different from those in many other languages. When English speakers talk about subjects in general, they use either the singular or plural *indefinite* form. The definite article *the* is not used.

examples: We should not let *children* with brain damage die.
We should not let a *child* with brain damage die.

With noncount nouns, no article is used.

> *example:* Through modern *technology*, many children are kept alive.

Which of these nouns are noncount? Put a check (√) next to each. On a separate page, write sentences using each of the nouns with a general meaning.

> *example:* There are special schools for children that have mental retardation.

1. mental retardation
2. research
3. hospital
4. machine
5. life

6. baby
7. brain damage
8. doctor
9. parent
10. operation

4. Writing the First Draft

Write your composition. Use your introduction and example with its transition sentence. Use restrictive adjective clauses and quotations if you can. Write on every other line so you can revise your paragraph easily.

5. Editing Practice

Using *the* in Sentences with *of* + Noun Phrase

The article *the* appears before specific nouns—people, places, or things that are one of a kind (*the earth*), already mentioned (*the patient in the hospital we talked about*), or members of a group (*the doctors at St. Joseph's Hospital*). It is also used before a noun followed by *of* + noun phrase.

> noun phrase
>
> *example:* I am against the use of life-support systems.

The noun *use* is specified in this sentence by *of* + the noun phrase that follows it.

 **exercise 1**   For the nouns below, write sentences with *of* + noun phrases. Put *the* in the correct places. The first one is done as an example.

    1. importance of good health

    The importance of good health should never be forgotten.

    2. worth of an individual's life

    _____

    3. courage of the dying man

    _____

    4. preservation of individual rights

    _____

    _____

 **exercise 2**   Here are the first paragraphs of the composition on page 148. Edit them and rewrite them correctly. Check the use of indefinite forms when marking generalizations. Also, check for the use of *the* in sentences with *of* + noun phrases. Then compare it with the composition on page 148.

        People on life-support machines are all different and in different situations. For that and other reasons, I believe family and doctor of patient on a life-support machine should be able to decide whether to remove the person from the machine or not. If the person on the machine is able to participate in decision, he or she should definitely have the right to choose.

        With a modern technology, it is very difficult to determine what is real life and what is artificial life. Is a person who is breathing with help of a machine but whose brain is dead really alive or not? No one can say for sure because each individual situation is different.

        I recently saw a program on TV that illustrates how the government's interference causes the great suffering. A machine was breathing for a man who was dying of cancer and he wanted to be removed from it. He said, "I want to live, but not tied to machine." When he tried to turn off machine himself, the doctors tied his hands to the bed because they thought the government would sue them if man died. I think it is wrong to ignore the patience wishes.

6. Editing Your Writing

Edit your composition using the checklist below. First, check it for content, organization, cohesion, and style using items 1, 2, and 3 in the checklist. Then edit your composition for grammar and form using items 4 and 5.

> ### Editing Checklist
>
> 1. Content
>   a. Did you support your opinion with good reasons and information?
>   b. Is your composition interesting?
> 2. Organization
>   a. Do you have an introduction, supporting paragraphs, and a conclusion?
>   b. Is your focus clear?
>   c. Did you give examples to support your reasons?
> 3. Cohesion and Style
>   a. Did you introduce your examples with transitions?
>   b. Did you use quotations to support your argument?
> 4. Grammar
>   a. Did you use indefinite forms correctly?
>   b. Did you use *the* correctly in sentences with *of* + noun phrases?
> 5. Form
>   a. Did you use correct essay form? (introduction, three supporting paragraphs, and a conclusion)
>   b. Did you use correct paragraph format? (indentation, division of words between syllables, margins)
>   c. Did you use correct punctuation? (capitalization, commas, periods)
>   d. Did you check the spelling of the words you are not sure of?

Exchange papers with another classmate and edit each other's compositions. Circle or underline in pencil any words, phrases, or sentences that you don't understand or that you think need to be corrected. Then return your compositions. Discuss any questions you have with your partner.

7. Writing the Second Draft

After you edit your composition, rewrite it neatly, using good handwriting and correct form. Then give your composition to your teacher for comments.

A STEP beyond

activity 1

Have a debate on the question you wrote about. The class will divide into two teams, with one team taking the affirmative side and one the negative side.

First meet with the members of your team and read each others' compositions. Make a list of your arguments. Then try to guess what the other team will argue and think of reasons against their arguments (rebuttals).

Choose three students to represent each side. One will give the arguments (about five minutes), one the rebuttal (about three minutes), and one the summary (about three minutes).

activity 2

Find a persuasive article in the editorial section of your local newspaper. With a partner, outline the article. How many paragraphs does it have? Is there an introductory paragraph? How many reasons for his or her opinion does the author present? What examples does the author use? Are you persuaded by his or her argument? Why or why not?

activity 3

Write a three-paragraph essay taking the opposite side of the question you wrote about for this chapter. You may get opposite points of view by recalling what the other side said during the debate you held or by interviewing a classmate who disagrees with you.

Journal Writing

activity 4

Write for fifteen minutes about one of the following topics.

1. Write about a person who has overcome a great handicap. It can be someone you know or a famous person.
2. Write in your journal on any topic you choose.

CHAPTER eleven

The Media

in this chapter

You are going to write a newspaper article.

STEPS TO **WRITING**

1. Exploring Ideas
Discussing a News Event

Look at the pictures of a flood and an earthquake. Discuss what information you would expect to find in an article about each event.

Write five questions you would expect each article to answer.

THE FLOOD

1. _____

2. _____

3. _____

4. _____

5. _____

THE EARTHQUAKE

1. _____
   _____

2. _____
   _____

3. _____
   _____

4. _____
   _____

5. _____
   _____

exercise **3**   In this chapter you are going to write a short article about a fire. Write five questions you would expect an article to answer about the fire in the picture below.

1. _____
   _____

2. _____
   _____

3. _____
   _____

4. _____
   _____

5. _____
   _____

WHAT DO YOU THINK?

Distinguishing Fact from Opinion

When a reporter writes an article about an event, he or she usually gives only facts. It is not appropriate for reporters to give their personal opinions or to include information that may or may not be correct.

Practice distinguishing fact from opinion. Read the following paragraph. Draw a line through any information that should not be included—information that is the reporter's opinion and not fact. When you finish, compare your results with a partner.

FUMES FROM CHEMICAL PLANT SEND DOZENS TO HOSPITAL

A cloud of sulfuric acid fumes sickened thirty-six people as it swept across downtown Middleport yesterday. The poisonous cloud came from the Kozar Chemical Plant in Santa Clara, California, which should be closed. Officials at the plant say that the sulfuric acid escaped as it was being transferred from one tank to another. I think this was very careless of the plant workers. Two weeks ago there was a similar accident at this plant. Most people believe that the plant officials should be fired for their carelessness.

Building Vocabulary

Add to this list any new vocabulary or expressions from your discussion and questions.

NOUNS	VERBS	ADJECTIVES	OTHER
blaze	break out	burned	overcome by
fire company	injure	burning	smoke
firefighters	rescue	heroic	
firetruck	save	hospitalized	_____

NOUNS	VERBS	ADJECTIVES	OTHER
flames	trap	injured	_____
hero, heroine			
(the) injured	_____	_____	_____
injury			
smoke	_____	_____	_____
victim			
_____	_____	_____	_____
_____	_____	_____	_____

2. Organizing Ideas

Answering Questions in an Article About an Event

> The first paragraph of an article gives you the most important facts. It usually answers these questions, sometimes called the five Ws.
>
> Who?   What?   Where?   When?   Why?

 Read the following article. Then underline the words that answer the questions above.

MAN AND TWO BOYS MISSING OFF CAPE COD

A 65-year-old man, his ten-year-old grandson, and another boy were missing yesterday after their empty boat was found off Cape Cod, the Coast Guard said. Police and Coast Guard units, which included two helicopters and four boats, searched through the night for the missing man and boys. The missing were Joseph Miller, a retired teacher, his grandson Eric Miller, and Eric's friend Anthony Blondell, 9, all from Northport, Florida. Anthony's father, John Blondell, said that Mr. Miller took the boys fishing with him on Friday morning. When the three did not return home by dark, Miller's daughter-in-law

A Coast Guard search unit

called the police. Miller's empty boat was found at about 11:00 A.M. yesterday, approximately one mile from Cape Cod. Coast Guard investigators say they have no idea what happened to the three.

"All Joe wanted to do was go fishing," said Rick Mendoza, 48, a close friend of Miller's and the last one to see the man and the boys alive.

 Imagine that there has been a fire somewhere at your school. Record information about this imaginary fire for your article. Answer these questions:

1. Who?_____

_____

2. What? _____

_____

3. Where? _____

_____

4. When?_____

_____

5. Why?_____

_____

Adding a Title

> The titles of stories for newspapers and magazines must get the readers' attention in as few words as possible. Therefore the verb *be* and articles are often omitted.
>
> > *Fact:* A man was killed by a hit and run driver.
> > *Title:* Man Killed by Hit and Run Driver
> > *Fact:* A hurricane is approaching the East Coast.
> > *Title:* Hurricane Approaching East Coast
> > *Fact:* First National Bank was robbed by a man in a Santa Claus suit.
> > *Title:* First National Bank Robbed by Man in Santa Claus Suit

 Rewrite these sentences as titles; omit any unnecessary words.

1. A provincial capital was taken over by guerrillas.

_____

2. The Waldorf Art Museum was destroyed by an explosion.

_____

3. Four people were killed in a plane crash.

_____

4. Killer bees are threatening cattle in Texas.

_____

5. A convicted murderer was executed.

_____

 Write a title for your article. _____

3. Developing Cohesion and Style

Using Relative Clauses (Review)

Read this paragraph.

> There was a fire in Middletown yesterday. It started in a warehouse and quickly spread to three nearby stores. The fire burned for four hours. The fire did $100,000 worth of damage. The fire killed one security guard and injured another.

The paragraph would sound much better if its five short sentences were combined into two longer sentences.

> A fire that started in a Middletown warehouse yesterday and quickly spread to three nearby stores did $100,000 worth of damage. The fire, which burned for four hours, killed one security guard and injured another.

Note that the combined sentences contain two different kinds of relative clauses. The relative clause in the first sentence does not have commas before and after it. This type of clause is called a restrictive relative clause. It contains information that is essential to the sentence and identifies the noun modified by answering the question "which one?"

The second type of relative clause is called a nonrestrictive relative clause. The information in a nonrestrictive relative clause is not essential to the sentence; it is set off by commas.

Using Restrictive Relative Clauses: Review

 **exercise 1** Combine the information in these sentences, using restrictive relative clauses.

   1. A seventeen-year-old girl is in critical condition at Long Island Hospital. She was hit by a car last night.

   _____

   _____

   2. A volcano erupted on the island of Hawaii yesterday. It has destroyed ten homes.

   _____

   _____

   3. Three children escaped without injury from their burning home. They were playing with matches.

   _____

   _____

   4. The miners' strike will be settled this week. It has paralyzed Britain's coal industry.

   _____

   _____

   5. A policeman wounded a robber. The robber was trying to steal an elderly woman's purse.

   _____

   _____

Using Nonrestrictive Relative Clauses

exercise 2 Combine the information in these sentences, using nonrestrictive relative clauses beginning with who, which, whose, where, or when. Remember to set off the clause with commas. (For information on punctuating relative clauses, see Appendix Three.)

   1. Tracy O'Brian was crossing Wantaugh Avenue at the time of the accident. She was a senior at Wantaugh High School.

   _____

   _____

2. The volcano has erupted several times in recent years. It is one of the most active volcanoes in the world.

_____

_____

3. The children were rescued by a neighbor. The children's mother was at the store.

_____

_____

4. Brian McDonald said that he believes the miners will go back to work next week. Brian McDonald is the head of the Miners' Union.

_____

_____

5. The elderly woman was rushed to Fairfield Hospital. The elderly woman had tried to fight off her attacker.

_____

_____

6. On Christmas Day two gunmen tried to rob a bank. On this day, most people are at home with their families.

_____

_____

7. In Thailand two tourists were arrested for sitting on the head of a statue of Buddha. In Thailand most people are Buddhists.

_____

_____

 *exercise* **3**   Rewrite this paragraph on a separate page. Combine the sentences within parentheses, using restrictive and nonrestrictive relative clauses.

(A tugboat disappeared off the Connecticut coast yesterday. The tugboat carried six crew members.) (The boat left Bridgeport harbor at 8:00 P.M. on Saturday. The tugboat was on its way out to sea.) (A helicopter was sent in search of the tugboat. The tugboat was supposed to arrive on Saturday night.) (The president of the tugboat company said that they will not stop searching until the tugboat is found. The president's son is aboard the tugboat.)

 **exercise 4**

Look at the information you wrote for your paragraph. Write three sentences using restrictive and/or nonrestrictive relative clauses.

_____

_____

_____

_____

_____

_____

focus on testing

Checking for Mechanics

Checking for mechanics in your writing means checking for punctuation and capitalization, spelling, and handwriting. These things may not have much to do with organizing and developing ideas, but they make your writing a lot easier to read. When you take a timed test, always leave a few minutes at the end to check for mechanics. Try looking for one thing at a time (punctuation/capitalization, spelling, or handwriting). Also, try reading your essay backwards—that is, read the last sentence first, then the second-to-last, etc. This makes mechanical mistakes easier to find.

4. Writing the First Draft

Write your article using the questions you wrote in Exercise 3 in Exploring Ideas. Use relative clauses and be careful to omit unnecessary words. Write on every other line so you can revise your paragraph easily.

5. Editing Practice
Using Commas
with Nonrestrictive Clauses

 **exercise 1**

Edit this article for the use of commas with nonrestrictive clauses.

Janet Reese a ten-year-old burn victim who was set on fire by her mother two years ago wants to help other child-abuse victims around the country. She is being treated at the Miami Burn Center and says that other children, who have gone through similar experiences, can get encouragement from her experience.

Specialists at the Burn Center a team of doctors and nurses who are among the best in the country are impressed by her courage and determination. The doctor, who is treating her, said that her courage and will to live were the things that really kept her alive.

Janet is sending letters to other burn patients, who are victims of child abuse. She tells them that she was hurt, but she got better, and they can too.

Using Reduced Clauses

Good writers generally try to use as few words as possible. Therefore, they often leave out unnecessary words in relative clauses. Here are two ways to do this:

1. You can omit the relative pronoun if it refers to the *object* of a restrictive relative clause.

    example: The man *that the policeman caught* was wearing a Santa Claus suit. →
    The man the policeman caught was wearing a Santa Claus suit.

2. You can omit the pronoun and the auxiliary verb *be* in restrictive and nonrestrictive relative clauses.

    examples: First National Bank, *which is protected by Benson Security,* was robbed yesterday. →
    First National Bank, protected by Benson Security, was robbed yesterday.

    The girl *who was missing for two days* was found unharmed. →
    The girl missing for two days was found unharmed.

    Several firefighters *who were on the scene* were overcome by smoke. →
    Several firefighters on the scene were overcome by smoke.

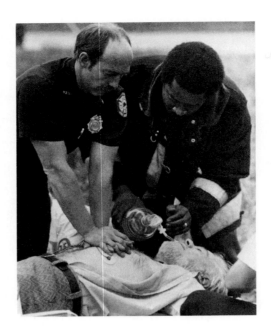

 **exercise 2**

Read this paragraph and omit any unnecessary words.

FIRE IN CAMERON HOTEL

A two-alarm fire broke out on the sixth floor of the beautiful and expensive Cameron Hotel early yesterday. The fire, which was controlled by firefighters after four hours, caused extensive damage to the hotel, although no serious injuries were reported. The blaze started in a resident's room of the twelve-story hotel at 222 W. 23rd Street shortly after 3:00 A.M. Someone said that the blaze was caused by a guest who was smoking in bed. While they struggled to control the flames, four firefighters were overcome by smoke and taken to Roosevelt Hospital. Fire officials who were on the scene said that there will be an official investigation into the cause of the fire.

exercise 3

Look at the sentences you wrote for your article. Are there any words that can be omitted?

6. Editing Your Writing

 **exercise 1**

Edit your article using the checklist on the next page. First, check your paragraph for content, organization, cohesion and style using items 1, 2, and 3 in the checklist. Then edit your paragraph for grammar and form using items 4 and 5.

Editing Checklist

1. Content
   a. Is your article interesting?
   b. Does it provide enough detail?
2. Organization
   a. Does your article answer the questions. Who? What? Where? When? Why?
   b. Did you have an appropriate title?
   c. Did you include facts and not personal opinions?
3. Cohesion and Style
   a. Did you use restrictive relative clauses correctly?
   b. Did you use nonrestrictive relative clauses correctly?
4. Grammar
   a. Did you punctuate relative clauses correctly?
   b. Did you use correct verb tenses?
5. Form
   a. Did you use correct paragraph format? (indentation, division of words between syllables, margins)
   b. Did you use correct punctuation? (capitalization, commas, periods)
   c. Did you check the spelling of the words you are not sure of?

Exchange papers with another classmate and edit each other's articles. Circle or underline in pencil any words, phrases, or sentences that you don't understand or that you think need to be corrected. Then return your articles. Discuss any questions you have with your partner.

7. Writing the Second Draft

After you edit your article, rewrite it neatly, using good handwriting and form. Then give your article to your teacher for comments.

A STEP **beyond**

Make a school newspaper. Choose some of the articles about the fire. Also write some other articles about anything interesting that has happened to the students at your school. You can write about accidents, important events, sports, family life, or achievements.

activity **2**   Find an article in a newspaper or a magazine on a subject that interests you. Try to find one that has three or more paragraphs. Read the article carefully. Then, without looking at it, summarize the information in the article in *one* sentence. (*Hint:* Answer as many of the *wh-* questions—"Who?" "What?" etc.—as you can in one well-written sentence.) Then expand your one-sentence summary to *one* paragraph. Exchange your work with a classmate. Give him or her the sentence to read first, then the paragraph, and, finally, the original article.

Journal Writing

activity **3**   Write for fifteen minutes about the following topics.

1. Write about the most frightening experience you have ever had.
2. Write about the saddest experience you have ever had.
3. Write about the happiest experience you have ever had.

With a partner, discuss the journal writing topics above. Which was the easiest to write? Why? Which was the most difficult? Why? For which experience could you remember the most details? Why?

CHAPTER twelve

Prejudice, Tolerance, and Justice

You are going to write a proposal to solve a community problem.

in this chapter

STEPS TO **writing**

1. Exploring Ideas
Discussing Community Problems

 **exercise 1**

Discuss the pictures on pages 173 to 175. Each one shows a solution to a problem. What problem is represented by each picture?

 exercise 2

List on the board some problems that people in your community or school have. Then choose a problem you are interested in and discuss possible solutions in small groups. Try to think of as many solutions as you can.

 **exercise 3**

Choose a problem and write a proposal. Begin by proposing a solution to the problem. Use the word should to propose your solution. Then give one or two reasons that show who would benefit from your proposal. Use the words would, might, or could to give your reasons.

example: Webster College should have an English-tutoring program for international students. This tutorial program would benefit students who need extra help with their English, especially with writing. These students might get better grades as a result of this program.

Write your proposal on the lines.

_____

_____

_____

_____

WHAT DO YOU THINK?

Determining Realistic Solutions

It's easy to think of solutions to problems, but a good solution is one that is realistic—that is, one that will work in the real world. Take a major city that has a serious air pollution problem, for example. Someone might propose closing downtown streets to car traffic as a means to cleaner air. But is this a realistic solution? What about people who must drive in order to earn their living? What about delivery trucks? What about businesses that service cars and trucks? Are people going to like this solution? Probably not. Asking questions like these about a solution to a problem can help you decide whether it is realistic.

Practice this skill with a partner by proposing solutions to the following problems. Then evaluate each others' solutions by asking questions like the preceding ones.

- Students are complaining about the food served in the school cafeteria.
- A teacher is not teaching what is in the syllabus.
- A foreign language class has 45 students in it; the students feel they are not getting enough individual attention.
- Students are complaining about people skateboarding around campus during school hours.

A new day-care center for the students and staff of a local community college

New low-cost housing for city residents

A cafeteria whose menu has been changed to include foods its international students have requested

Volunteer tutor from home for the aged tutoring student from nearby school

 **exercise 4** Write two to four reasons why you think that your proposal is a good one.

1. _____

2. _____

3. _____

4. _____

Building Vocabulary

exercise 5 Add new vocabulary from your discussion to this list.

NOUNS	VERBS	ADJECTIVES	OTHER
advantage	benefit	beneficial	_____
benefit	establish	expensive	_____
disadvantage	give ____ a	realistic	_____
establishment	chance		_____
expense	improve		
improvement	organize	_____	_____
organization	raise objections	_____	_____
_____	_____	_____	_____
_____	_____	_____	_____
_____	_____	_____	_____

2. Organizing Ideas

Determining Who Your Audience Is

You are going to write a persuasive essay. In your essay, you will try to convince a group of people that your proposal is a good one. The arguments that you use will depend on who your audience is. For example, if you think that the classes in your school should be limited to twelve students, you will have to try to convince the school administration. If you think that students who speak a language other than English in the classroom should be fined, you will have to convince your classmates and your teacher.

 **exercise 1**   Who is the audience for your essay? _____

_____

Countering Objections to Your Proposal

Once you know who your audience is, you will have to try to think of some objections that they may have to your proposal. You will have to imagine what their viewpoint is. For example, in answer to a proposal that classes in your school should be limited to twelve students, the school administrators might have these two objections:

1. There is no money to hire more teachers.
2. There are not enough classrooms to divide the classes.

To convince the administration that classes should be smaller, you will have to counter these objections. The best way to do this is to provide possible solutions to the objections.

 **exercise 2**   In small groups, discuss some possible solutions to the administration's two objections. Write down your solutions. Then join another group of students. Compare your solutions. Are they similar or different? Which solutions are most realistic?

 **exercise 3**   Look at this proposal:

> Students who speak their native language in the classroom should be fined 25 cents.

exercise **4**   List two possible objections to this proposal.

1. _____

2. _____

exercise **5**   List counterarguments to these objections.

1. _____

2. _____

exercise **6**   Now list some objections that your audience might have to your proposal.

1. _____

2. _____

3. _____

4. _____

exercise **7**   List possible counterarguments to these objections.

1. _____

2. _____

3. _____

4. _____

Making an Outline

Your composition will include an introductory paragraph and a closing paragraph. In addition, there will be one paragraph for each of your arguments and a paragraph listing possible objections and countering them. It is often easier to organize this type of writing by putting it in a simplified outline form:

   I. Introductory paragraph: states proposal and lists arguments for it
  II. Persuasive argument 1: develops the first argument and says why your proposal should be carried out
 III. Persuasive argument 2: develops the second argument
 IV. Counterarguments: counters objections
  V. Concluding paragraph: summarizes reasons for the solution you proposed

Here is a sample outline.

  I. Introductory paragraph
      1. ABC English Language Academy should start a cooperative day-care center.
      2. It would benefit both the community and the school.

  II. Argument 1
      1. It would benefit the community:
         a. Mothers of young children cannot attend English classes because they cannot afford to hire babysitters.
         b. Many women have no chance to learn English and feel uncomfortable living in the United States.
         c. Their children do not learn English until they go to school.
         d. Mothers cannot help children with their schoolwork because of the language barrier.

  III. Argument 2
      1. It would benefit the school:
         a. People would feel that the school was really interested in helping the community (public relations).
         b. Staff members could have good day care for their children.
         c. It would help attract a better staff.
         d. It would make the staff feel more content.
         e. School enrollment would increase.

  IV. Counterarguments
      1. To the objection that it would be difficult for the school to organize:
         a. A student-staff organizing committee could be created.
         b. Several interested students and staff members have experience working in day-care centers.
         c. The committee would take complete responsibility for obtaining licenses and other such tasks.
      2. To the objection that it would cost the school too much money:
         a. Because it would be a cooperative, students and staff would volunteer their time.
         b. Participating students and staff members could bring in used toys, books, etc.
         c. A small enrollment fee could be used to cover the cost of furniture and other necessary items.
         d. There is a possibility that the government would help fund the center.

  V. Concluding paragraph

exercise 8 Now make a similar outline for your essay. Your essay may have from four to six paragraphs. Just remember that each separate argument should be stated in a new paragraph.

focus on testing

Making an Outline

Exercise 8, above, asks you to make an outline for your essay. It's just as important to make an outline when you have to take a timed test. You will have less time in a testing situation, so you will have to make a less *complete* outline than you would at home. However, having at least the following will make your writing task a lot easier:

- A statement of the main idea of the entire essay—this will be in your introductory paragraph.
- A list of ideas to support your main idea—these will be the topic sentences of each of your body paragraphs.
- Two or more examples for each supporting idea—these will develop each of your body paragraphs.

3. Developing Cohesion and Style

Using the Conditional Mood

Do these sentences refer to conditions that presently exist or to conditions that might or could exist *if* something else were true?

1. If I were rich, I *would* buy a Mercedes Benz.
2. If you paid attention in class, you *could* learn to speak English.
3. If Ricardo tried jogging, he *might* lose weight.

In your essay, you will probably have to use the auxiliaries *would, could,* and *might* because your arguments, objections, and counter-arguments will be based on the condition that your proposal is accepted. For example, suppose that your proposal is:

Class size should be limited to twelve students.

The condition "if class size were limited to twelve students" will be the basis of your entire composition, even if it is not written with each sentence. Note that in this conditional sentence, *were* is used with a singular subject (class size).

example: (if class size were limited to twelve students) The teachers **would** be able to spend more time with each student. In addition, (if the class size were limited to twelve students) the students **might** get to know each other better. Finally, (if the class size were limited to twelve students) students **could** practice speaking more.

 **exercise 1** Read the following paragraph. Complete it by circling the correct modal auxiliary. Remember to use *would, could,* or *might* when there is a condition that is not presently true or real.

I believe that students in our class should be fined for speaking their native language during class time. This (*will* / *would*) have several benefits. First of all, students (*will* / *would*) learn to rely on English more. Second, students who don't speak the same native language (*might* / *can*) get to know each other better. Third, students (*will* / *would*) be more likely to tell the teacher when they are having problems. Finally, we (*can* / *could*) use the money from the fines to have a party at the end of the semester.

Using Linking Expressions and Transition Words for Listing Ideas

Most of your essay will consist of lists. There will be a list of arguments in favor of your proposal, a list of possible objections, and a list of counterarguments to the objections. Since there are so many places where you will have to list or enumerate ideas, it is important to try to use several different linking expressions and transition words. You can use these expressions at the beginning of each new paragraph and within the paragraphs themselves.

Suppose that the first idea in your essay is the following: A day-care center would benefit the community by making it possible for mothers of young children to attend class. Here are some of the most common ways to add ideas to your composition using linking expressions.

linking expressions	examples of additional ideas
also	It would *also* benefit the school . . . Another *benefit* would be that . . .
at the same time	*At the same time,* teachers would benefit.
besides + noun *or* noun phrase	*Besides benefiting* the community, it would benefit the school. (*Besides this,* it would benefit the school.)
furthermore	*Furthermore,* the school would benefit.
in addition	*In addition,* the school would benefit.
moreover	*Moreover,* the school would benefit.
similarly	*Similarly,* it would benefit the school.

Here are some common transition words for listing ideas in order.

transition words	examples
first (of all)	*First of all,* mothers of young children would be able to attend classes.
second	*Second,* school staff members would be able to use the center.
finally	*Finally,* the school would also receive many benefits from this type of program.

exercise  Complete the following paragraph with transition words and linking expressions; choose from those given in this section. Add punctuation where necessary.

There are several ways that the community would benefit from the establishment of a day-care center. _____ it would give non-English speakers a chance to go to school to learn English, and they would become more integrated into the life of the community. _____ improving community relations, a day-care center would help non-English-speaking parents raise their standard of living because, if they learned English, they could get better jobs. _____ the parents would be able to help their children with their schoolwork and communicate with their teachers.

_____ a day-care center would give non-English-speaking children and English-speaking children a chance to get to know each other.

_____ all parents (not just non-English speakers) would have a place to leave their children while they work.

Using Connecting Words and Transitions for Contrasting Ideas and Showing Cause and Result: Review

In your second-to-last paragraph, you will list possible objections and then counter them. To do this, you will need to review some of the connecting words and transitions you have already learned.

CONNECTING WORDS AND TRANSITIONS FOR CONTRASTING IDEAS

although	even though	nevertheless
but	however	while

CONNECTING WORDS AND TRANSITIONS FOR SHOWING CAUSE AND RESULT

as a result	consequently	so
because	since	therefore

 Complete the following paragraph by circling the correct connecting words or transitions.

Several objections to a day-care center may be raised. First of all, some people may say that it is impossible (*because / although*) it would be difficult to organize. (*However / Therefore*), there are several students and staff members
1   2
who have day-care experience and are willing to set it up. Another objection might be that it would be expensive (*while / so*) the school would have to raise
3
tuition. (*Consequently / But*) this is not necessarily true. (*Since / Although*) there
4   5
would be some initial expense, it can be kept to a minimum by having partici-pants donate used toys and books and pay a small enrollment fee.

Writing a Concluding Paragraph

 Read this concluding paragraph and then answer the following questions about it.

In conclusion, because of the benefits to both the school and the commu-nity, the advantages of a day-care center clearly outweigh the disadvantages; therefore, I hope that the school administration will consider this proposal carefully.

1. What transition expression does the paragraph begin with? (Other possible concluding expressions are *in summary* and *to conclude*.)
2. Did the writer restate the ideas in different words?
3. How did the writer end the concluding paragraph? Did the writer use *will* or *would* after the verb *hope*?

4. Writing the First Draft

Write your essay using the outline you made. Remember to use transitions and connecting words in the essay. Write on every other line so you can revise your paragraphs easily.

5. Editing Practice

Edit this paragraph for all errors, and rewrite it correctly. Then check it against the paragraph on page 182.

There is several way that the community would beneficial from establishment of day-care center. First, it would give non-English speakers a chance to go to school to learn English, and they will become more integrated into the life of the community. Besides improve community relations, a day-care center will help non-English-speaking parents raise their standard of living because, if they learned English, they can get better jobs. Also, parent would be able to help their children with their schoolwork and communicate with their teachers. Moreover, a day-care center gives non-English-speaking children and English-speaking children a chance to get to know one another. Finally, all parents (not just non-English speakers) would have a place to leave its child while they work.

6. Editing Your Writing

Edit your essay using the checklist below. First, check your essay for content, organization, cohesion, and style using items 1, 2, and 3 in the checklist. Then edit it for grammar and form using items 4 and 5.

Editing Checklist

1. Content
   a. Did you state the problem correctly?
   b. Did you give reasons for your proposal?
2. Organization
   a. Are your arguments appropriate for your audience?
   b. Did you counter any possible objections?

3. Cohesion and Style
    a. Did you use the transition words for contrasting ideas correctly?
    b. Did you use transition words for enumerating ideas correctly?
4. Grammar
    Did you use the conditional mood correctly?
5. Form
    a. Did you use correct paragraph format? (indentation, division of words between syllables, margins)
    b. Did you use correct punctuation? (capitalization, commas, periods)
    c. Did you check the spelling of the words you are not sure of?

Exchange papers with another classmate and edit each other's essays. Circle or underline in pencil any words, phrases, or sentences that you don't understand or that you think need to be corrected. Then return your essays. Discuss any questions you have with your partner.

7. Writing the Second Draft

After you edit your essay, rewrite it neatly, using good handwriting and correct form.

A STEP beyond

Present your essay to the class as a speech. First, write the main ideas and important phrases on notecards. Then, on your own, practice giving the speech. Speak slowly and stress important words. Pause between phrases. Get to know the speech so that you can look at the audience while you speak.

activity 2   Look at the paragraph on page 180 on fining students for speaking their native language during class time. You are going to expand this paragraph into a six-paragraph essay. Work in small groups. Begin by outlining the four arguments the author presents. Then suggest details and examples to further develop each of the four arguments. Finally, write out the new essay, including introductory and concluding paragraphs.

activity 3   Working on your own, write a four- to six-paragraph essay taking the opposite side of the English-only issue presented in the preceding activity. (Or take the opposite side of your own essay that you wrote for this chapter.)

activity 4   Find articles in newspapers and magazines on the "English-Only" movement in the United States. (Use the *Readers' Guide to Periodical Literature* or an electronic database in the library to find the articles. Look under the heading of "English Only"—the librarian will help you.) Bring copies of these articles to class and discuss them with your classmates. What are some of the arguments of the proponents (the people who are *for* the issue)? What are the opposing viewpoints? What is your opinion?

Journal Writing

activity 5   Write for fifteen minutes about the following topics.

1. Write about the most important issue or problem facing you in your life at this moment.
2. Write on a possible solution to the problem or issue you described in the preceding activity.

activity 6   Since this is the end of the course, you should now do a self-evaluation. Look at the comments your teacher has given you throughout the course and answer these questions.

1. How have you improved?
2. What are your strong points?
3. What are your weak points?
4. What should you be especially careful of when you revise?
5. What should you be especially careful of when you edit?
6. How do you feel about writing in English now?

Appendixes

Spelling Rules for Adding Endings

Rules for Adding Endings That Begin with Vowels (-*ed, ing, -er, -est*)

1. For Words ending in a silent *e*, drop the *e* and add the ending.

   like → lik**ed**   make → mak**ing**   safe → saf**er**   fine → fin**est**

2. For one-syllable words ending in a single vowel and a single consonant, double the final consonant.

   bat → bat**ted**   run → run**ning**   fat → fat**ter**   hot → hot**test**

3. Don't double the final consonant when the word has two final consonants or two vowels before a final consonant.

   pick → pick**ed**   sing → sing**ing**   clean → clean**er**
   cool → cool**est**

4. For words of two or more syllables that end in a single vowel and a single consonant, double the final consonant if the word is accented on the final syllable.

   refer′→ refer**red**   impel′ → impel**led**

5. For words of two or more syllables that end in a single vowel and single consonant, make no change if the word isn't accented on the final syllable.

   tra′vel → travel**ed**   fo′cus → focus**ed**

6. For words ending in a consonant and *y,* change the *y* to *i* and add the ending *unless the ending begins with i.*

   study → stud**ied**   dirty → dirt**ier**   sunny → sunn**iest**
   study → study**ing**   hurry → hurry**ing**

7. For words ending in a vowel and *y,* make no change before adding the ending.

   play → play**ed**   stay → stay**ing**

Rules for Adding Endings That Begin with Consonants (-*ly, -ment*)

8. For words ending in a silent *e*, make no change when adding endings that begin with consonants.

   fine → fine**ly**   state → state**ment**

9. For words ending in a consonant and *y,* change the *y* to *i* before adding the ending.

   happy → happ**ily**   merry → merr**iment**

Rules for Adding a Final *s* to Nouns and Verbs

10. Generally, add the s without making changes.

     sit → sit**s**   dance → dance**s**   play → play**s**   book → book**s**

11. If a word ends in a consonant and *y,* change the *y* to *i* and add *es.*

     marry → marr**ies**   study → stud**ies**   cherry → cherr**ies**

12. If a word ends in *ch, s, sh, x,* or *z,* add *es:*

     church → church**es**   boss → boss**es**   mix → mix**es**
     cash → cash**es**   fizz → fizz**es**

13. For words ending in *o,* sometimes add *es* and sometimes add *s:*

     tomato → tomato**es**   potato → potato**es**
     piano → piano**s**   radio → radio**s**

14. For words ending in *f* or *fe,* generally drop the *f* for *fe* and add *ves:*

     knife → kni**ves**   wife → wi**ves**   life → li**ves**   loaf → loa**ves**

     Exceptions: safe → safe**s**   puff → puff**s**   roof → roof**s**

APPENDIX **two**

Capitalization Rules

First Words

1. Capitalize the first word of every sentence.

    They live in Rome.   **W**ho is it?

2. Capitalize the first word of a quotation.

    He said, "**M**y name is Paul."   Jenny asked, "**W**hen is the party?"

Personal Names

3. Capitalize names of people, including initials and titles of address.

    Mrs. **J**ones   **M**ohandas **G**andhi   **J**ohn **F**. **K**ennedy

4. Capitalize family words if used alone or followed by a name.

    Let's go, **D**ad.   Where's **G**randma?   She's at **A**unt **L**ucy's.

5. Don't capitalize family words if used with a possessive pronoun or article.

   my **u**ncle   her **m**other   our **g**randparents   an **a**unt

6. Capitalize the pronoun *I*.

   I have a book.   She's bigger than **I** am.

7. Capitalize names of God.

   God   **A**llah   **J**esus **C**hrist

8. Capitalize the names of nationalities, races, peoples, and religions.

   Arab   **A**sian   **C**hicano   **M**uslim

9. Generally, don't capitalize occupations.

   I am a secretary.   She wants to be a lawyer.

Place Names

10. Capitalize the names of countries, states, provinces, and cities.

   Mexico   **N**ew **Y**ork   **O**ntario   **T**okyo

11. Capitalize the names of oceans, lakes, rivers, islands, and mountains.

   the **A**tlantic **O**cean   **L**ake **C**omo   the **A**mazon
   Mt. **E**verest   **B**elle **I**sle

12. Capitalize the names of geographical areas.

   the **S**outh   the **E**ast **C**oast   **A**sia   **A**ntarctica

13. Don't capitalize directions if they aren't names of geographical areas.

   He lives **e**ast of Toronto.   They traveled **s**outhwest.

14. Capitalize names of schools, parks, buildings, and streets.

   the **U**niversity of **G**eorgia   **C**entral **P**ark
   the **S**ears **B**uilding   **O**xford **R**oad

Time Words

15. Capitalize names of days and months.

   Monday   **F**riday   **J**anuary   **M**arch

16. Capitalize names of holidays and historical events.

   Christmas   **N**ew **Y**ear's **D**ay   **I**ndependence **D**ay   **W**orld **W**ar II

17. Don't capitalize names of seasons.

   spring   summer   fall   winter

Titles

18. Capitalize the first word and all important words of titles of books, magazines, newspapers, and articles.

   Interactions   *Newsweek*   The *New York Times*   "**Rock Music Today**"

19. Capitalize the first word and all important words of names of movies, plays, radio programs, and television programs.

   The African Queen   *The Tempest*   "*News Roundup*"   "*Fame*"

20. Don't capitalize articles (*a, an, the*), conjunctions (*but, and, or*), and short prepositions (*of, with, in, on, for*) unless they are the first word of a title.

   The Life of Thomas Edison   *War and Peace*   *Death of a Salesman*

Names of Organizations

21. Capitalize the names of organizations, government groups, and businesses.

   International Student Association   the Senate   Gestetner

22. Capitalize trade names, but do not capitalize the name of the product.

   IBM typewriter   Toyota hatchback   Kellogg's cereal

Other

23. Capitalize the names of languages.

   Spanish   Thai   French   Japanese

24. Don't capitalize school subjects unless they are the names of languages or are followed by a number.

   geometry   music   English   Arabic   Biology 306

APPENDIX three

Punctuation Rules

Period

1. Use a period after a statement or command.

   We are studying English.   Open your books to Chapter Three.

2. Use a period after most abbreviations.

   Mr.   Ms.   Dr.   Ave.   etc.   U.S.

Exceptions: UN   NATO   IBM   AIDS

3. Use a period after initials.

    H. G. Wells   Dr. H. R. Hammond

Question Mark

4. Use a question mark after (not before) questions.

    Where are you going?   Is he here yet?

5. In a direct quotation, the question mark goes before the quotation marks.

    He asked, "What's your name?"

Exclamation Point

6. Use an exclamation point after exclamatory sentences or phrases.

    I won the lottery!   Be quiet!   Wow!

Comma

7. Use a comma before a conjunction (*and, or, so, but*) that separates two independent clauses.

    She wanted to go to work, so she decided to take an English course.
    He wasn't happy in that apartment, but he didn't have the money to move.

8. Don't use a comma before a conjunction that separates two phrases that aren't complete sentences.

    She worked in the library and studied at night.
    Do you want to go to a movie or stay home?

9. Use a comma after an introductory clause or phrase (generally if it is five or more words long)

    After a beautiful wedding ceremony, they had a reception in her mother's
       home.
    If you want to write well, you should practice writing almost every night.

10. Use a comma to separate interrupting expressions from the rest of a sentence.

    Do you know, by the way, what time dinner is?
    Many of the students, I found out, stayed on campus during the summer.

11. Use a comma after transitional expressions.

    In addition, he stole all her jewelry.
    However, he left the TV.

Common transitional expressions are:

therefore	moreover	however
consequently	furthermore	nevertheless
for this reason	besides	on the other hand
also	in fact	for example
in addition	similarly	for instance

12. Use a comma to separate names of people in direct address from the rest of a sentence.

Jane, have you seen Paul?
We aren't sure, Mrs. Shapiro, where he is.

13. Use a comma after *yes* and *no* in answers.

Yes, he was here a minute ago.
No, I haven't.

14. Use a comma to separate items in a series.

We have coffee, tea, and milk.
He looked in the refrigerator, on the shelves, and in the cupboard.

15. Use a comma to separate an appositive from the rest of a sentence.

Mrs. Sampson, his English teacher, gave him a good recommendation.
Would you like to try a taco, a delicious Mexican food?

16. If a date or address has two or more parts, use a comma after each part.

I was born on June 5, 1968.
The house at 230 Seventh Street, Miami, Florida, is for sale.

17. Use a comma to separate contrasting information from the rest of a sentence.

It wasn't Maria, but Parvin, who was absent.
Bring your writing book, not your reading book.

18. Use a comma to separate quoations from the rest of a sentence.

He asked, "What are we going to do?"
"I'm working downtown," he said,

19. Use a comma to separate two or more adjectives that each modify the noun alone.

She was an intelligent, beautiful actress. (*Intelligent* and *beautiful* both
    modify *actress*.)
Eat those delicious green beans. (*Delicious* modifies *green beans*.)

20. Use a comma to separate nonrestrictive clauses from the rest of a sentence. A clause is nonrestrictive if it isn't necessary to identify the noun modified. Clauses are usually nonrestrictive after:

a. proper names

Michael Jackson, who is now touring the country, is a famous rock star.

b. nouns that have already been identified

Tanya and Bertha Green were rescued from the fire. The girls, who are being treated at Midland Hospital, were badly injured.

c. nouns that can be identified because there is only one

The earth, which is the fifth largest planet, has one satellite.

21. Don't use commas after restrictive clauses. A restrictive clause is needed to identify the noun modified.

The firemen who rescued the two girls was given a medal.

Quotation Marks

22. Use quotation marks at the beginning and end of exact quotations. Other punctuation marks go before the end quotation marks.

He said, "I'm going to Montreal."
"How are you?" he asked.

23. Use quotation marks before and after titles of stories, articles, songs, and television programs. Periods and commas go before the final quotation marks, while question marks and exclamation points normally go after them.

Do you like to watch "Dallas" on television?
My favorite song is "Let It Be."
Do you like the story "Gift of the Magi"?

Apostrophe

24. Use apostrophes in contractions.

don't   it's   we've   they're

25. Use an apostrophe to make possessive nouns.

Singular: Jerry's   my boss's
Plural: the children's   the Smiths'

Underlining

26. Underline the titles of books, magazines, newspapers, plays, and movies.

I am reading <u>One Hundred Years of Solitude</u>.
Did you like the movie <u>It's a Wonderful Life</u>?

A List of Noncount Nouns

Food

bread, butter, cheese, chicken,* chocolate,* coffee,* cream, fish,* flour, fruit,* ice cream,* juice,* meat, milk,* rice, salt, spaghetti, sugar, tea

Natural Phenomena

Weather words: rain, snow,* sunshine, thunder, wind*
Gases: air, hydrogen, nitrogen, oxygen
Minerals: copper, gold, iron, silver, steel
Materials: dirt, dust, earth, grass, ice, land,* oil, sand, water*

Activities and Sports

baseball, * chess, dance,* skating, soccer, tennis

Emotions and Qualities†

ambition, anger, courage, fear, freedom, happiness, hatred, honesty, justice, loneliness, love, joy, pride

Social Issues†

abortion, crime, democracy, divorce, hunger, nuclear power, peace, pollution, poverty

Mass Nouns (Composed of Dissimilar Items)

change, clothing, fruit, equipment, furniture, jewelry, luggage, mail, machinery, makeup, medicine, money, noise, scenery, technology, transportation, vocabulary

---

*These nouns are sometimes count and sometimes noncount. They are noncount when they refer to the item in general. They are count when they refer to a particular item.

I like coffee and tea.
Please give me one coffee and two teas.

†Most emotions, qualities, and social issues can function as count nouns: *a strong ambition, a deep hatred, a terrible crime.*

Subjects

art,* economics, history,* humanities, physics

Miscellaneous

advice, business,* fun, glass,* homework, knowledge,* information, insurance, life, nature,* news, paint,* publicity, reality,* research, sleep, time,* traffic, trouble, tuition, work*

APPENDIX **five**

Subordinating Conjunctions

Subordinating conjunctions can show relationships of *time, reason, contrast,* and *purpose*.

1. Time: when, whenever, if
2. Reason: because, since
3. Contrast: although, even though, though
4. Purpose: so that

APPENDIX **six**

Transitions

Transitions are words or phrases that join two related ideas. Here is a list of the most common transitions.

1. Giving examples: for example, for instance
2. Adding emphasis: in fact, of course
3. Adding information: in addition, furthermore, moreover, besides
4. Making comparisons: similarly, likewise
5. Showing contrast: however, nevertheless, in contrast, on the contrary, on one hand/on the other hand
6. Giving reasons or results: therefore, as a result, as a consequence, for this (that) reason
7. Giving sequences: now, then, first (second, etc.), earlier, later, meanwhile, finally

Student Name _____ Date _____

Personal reaction

_____
_____
_____
_____

Chapter Checklist	<u>**Good**</u>	**Needs Work**

1. Content
   a. Did you include everything that you wanted to say?   ❑   ❑
   b. Did you give a reason for each opinion?   ❑   ❑

2. Organization
   a. Does your topic sentence give the main idea of your paragraph?   ❑   ❑
   b. Did you organize your ideas from most important to least important?   ❑   ❑

3. Cohesion and Style
   a. Did you use transition words and connectors?   ❑   ❑
   b. Did you use adverbs of frequency and quantifiers?   ❑   ❑

4. Grammar
   a. Did you use present tense verbs?   ❑   ❑
   b. Did you use adverbs of frequency and quanifiers?   ❑   ❑

5. Form
   a. Did you use correct paragraph format (indentation, division of words between syllables, margins)?   ❑   ❑
   b. Did you use correct punctuation (capitalization, commas, periods)?   ❑   ❑
   c. Did you check the spelling of words you were not sure of?   ❑   ❑

Other comments

_____
_____
_____
_____
_____
_____
_____
_____

Student Name _____ Date _____

Personal reaction

_____

_____

_____

_____

Chapter Checklist	**Good**	**Needs Work**
1. Content		
a. Did you add enough descriptive details?	❏	❏
b. Did you use a variety of adjectives?	❏	❏
2. Organization		
a. Is your topic sentence the main idea of your paragraph?	❏	❏
b. Do all the details develop the topic sentence?	❏	❏
c. Did you include a concluding sentence?	❏	❏
3. Cohesion and Style		
a. Have you given reasons for your feelings?	❏	❏
b. Have you varied word order of your sentences?	❏	❏
4. Grammar		
a. Did you avoid run-on sentences?	❏	❏
b. Did you use correct verb forms?	❏	❏
5. Form		
a. Did you use correct paragraph format (indentation, division of words between syllables, margins)?	❏	❏
b. Did you use correct punctuation (capitalization, commas, periods)?	❏	❏
c. Did you check the spelling of words you were not sure of?	❏	❏

Other comments

_____

_____

_____

_____

_____

_____

Student Name _____ Date _____

Personal reaction

_____

_____

_____

_____

Chapter Checklist   <u>Good</u>   <u>Needs Work</u>

1. Content
   a. Did you state your opinion clearly? ❑ ❑
   b. Did you support your opinion with reasons? ❑ ❑
   c. Did you support your reasons with examples and/or predictions? ❑ ❑
   d. Did you avoid faulty reasoning? ❑ ❑

2. Organization
   a. Did you write an opening sentence that told what article you are
      responding to and gave your opinion? ❑ ❑
   b. Did you write a concluding sentence? ❑ ❑

3. Cohesion and Style
   a. Did you use transitions? ❑ ❑
   b. Did you state your opinions using appropriate modals? ❑ ❑
   c. Did you use a moderate or a strong style to express your opinions? ❑ ❑

4. Grammar
   a. Did you use simple verb forms with modals? ❑ ❑
   b. Did you use present verb forms in *if* clauses and future verb forms
      in predictions? ❑ ❑
   c. Did you avoid run-on sentences? ❑ ❑

5. Form
   a. Did you use correct paragraph format (indentation, margins, capitals
      at beginning of sentences)? ❑ ❑
   b. Did you use correct spelling and syllabification? ❑ ❑

Other comments

_____

_____

_____

_____

_____

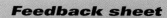
Student Name _____ Date _____

Personal reaction

_____
_____
_____
_____

Chapter Checklist	**Good**	**Needs Work**

1. Content
   a. Does your paragraph describe your best qualities? ❏ ❏
   b. Does it show that you can be successful in what you do? ❏ ❏
   c. Does it let the reader infer what your best qualities are? ❏ ❏

2. Organization
   a. Do you have too many ideas for one paragraph? Should you divide your paragraph into two paragraphs? ❏ ❏
   b. Are there any ideas not relevant to the topic? ❏ ❏
   c. Is your topic sentence positive? Does it make the reader want to find out more about you? ❏ ❏
   d. Does each sentence add a new idea? Should you take out or combine repetitive sentences? ❏ ❏
   e. Does your concluding sentence tell something you've learned or something you hope for in the future? ❏ ❏

3. Cohesion and Style
   a. Have you used verb tenses correctly? ❏ ❏
   b. Can you add demonstratives *(this, that, these, those)* and prepositional phrases with demonstratives to unify your paragraph? ❏ ❏

4. Grammar
   a. Are your verb forms correct? ❏ ❏
   b. Have you used run-on sentences or sentence fragments? ❏ ❏
   c. Have you used plural and singular demonstratives correctly? ❏ ❏

5. Form
   a. Is your capitalization correct? ❏ ❏
   b. Is your spelling of past participles correct? ❏ ❏

Other comments

_____
_____
_____

Student Name _____ Date _____

Personal reaction

_____
_____
_____
_____

Chapter Checklist	**Good**	**Needs Work**
1. Content		
a. Is your story interesting?	❏	❏
b. Does the lesson (conclusion) fit the story you told?	❏	❏
c. Have you given enough information?	❏	❏
2. Organization		
a. Have you avoided unimportant details and digressions?	❏	❏
b. Have you used paragraph divisions to make the story clearer?	❏	❏
3. Cohesion and Style		
a. Have you used transition words correctly?	❏	❏
b. Are your sentences in logical order?	❏	❏
4. Grammar		
Have you used the past, present perfect, and past perfect tenses correctly?	❏	❏
5. Form		
a. Did you use correct paragraph format (indentation, division of words between syllables, margins)?	❏	❏
b. Did you use correct punctuation (capitalization, commas, periods)?	❏	❏
c. Did you check the spelling of the words you are not sure of?	❏	❏

Other comments

_____
_____
_____
_____
_____
_____
_____
_____

Student Name _____   Date _____

Personal reaction

_____
_____
_____
_____

Chapter Checklist	<u>**Good**</u>	**Needs Work**
1. Content Does your paragraph give examples when necessary?	❏	❏
2. Organization Does your paragraph have a narrow-enough focus?	❏	❏
3. Cohesion and Style Have you used relative clauses correctly?	❏	❏
4. Grammar **a.** Have you used the correct part of speech for each word?	❏	❏
b. Have you used relative clauses correctly?	❏	❏
5. Form **a.** Have you used a capital letter to begin each sentence?	❏	❏
b. Have you used a period to end each sentence?	❏	❏
c. Have you punctuated relative clauses correctly?	❏	❏

Other comments

_____
_____
_____
_____
_____
_____
_____
_____
_____
_____
_____

CHAPTER seven

Feedback sheet

Student Name _____ Date _____

Personal reaction

_____

_____

_____

_____

Chapter Checklist	<u>**Good**</u>	**Needs Work**
1. Content		
a. Is the information interesting?	❏	❏
b. Does the composition answer most of the reader's questions?	❏	❏
2. Organization		
a. Are paragraphs organized chronologically?	❏	❏
b. Does your first paragraph have a good topic sentence?	❏	❏
c. Does your last paragraph have a concluding sentence?	❏	❏
3. Cohesion and Style		
a. Are your gerund and infinitive constructions parallel?	❏	❏
b. Did you use 'used to' too often?	❏	❏
4. Grammar		
a. Did you use *used to* and *would* correctly?	❏	❏
b. Did you use verbal adjectives correctly?	❏	❏
5. Form		
a. Did you use correct paragraph format (indentation, division of words between syllables, margins)?	❏	❏
b. Did you use correct punctuation (capitalization, commas, periods)?	❏	❏
c. Did you check the spelling of the words you are not sure of?	❏	❏

Other comments

_____

_____

_____

_____

_____

_____

_____

_____

Student Name _____ Date _____

Personal reaction

_____

_____

_____

_____

Chapter Checklist	<u>**Good**</u>	**Needs Work**

1. Content
  Does your composition list all the similarities and differences you
  think are important? ❏ ❏

2. Organization
  a. Does the topic sentence mention both similarities and differences even
    though it focuses on one or the other? ❏ ❏
  b. Does one paragraph deal with differences and the other with simi-
    larities? ❏ ❏

3. Cohesion and Style
  Have you used expressions as *both, neither, in contrast, on the other
  hand,* and *while?* ❏ ❏

4. Grammar
  a. Have you used gerunds correctly? ❏ ❏
  b. Have you used comparatives and superlatives correctly? ❏ ❏

5. Form
  a. Have you used a capital letter to begin each sentence? ❏ ❏
  b. Have you used a period to end each sentence? ❏ ❏

Other comments

_____

_____

_____

_____

_____

_____

_____

_____

Student Name _____ Date _____

Personal reaction

_____

_____

_____

_____

Chapter Checklist	<u>Good</u>	**Needs Work**
1. Content		
a. Is you information accurate?	❏	❏
b. Have you made interesting comparisons?	❏	❏
2. Organization		
Is the information organized logically?	❏	❏
3. Cohesion and Style		
a. Did you vary the word order in some sentences, using *with* + noun phrase, *because* and *because of?*	❏	❏
b. Did you use *unlike* + noun phrase to show contrast?	❏	❏
4. Grammar		
a. Did you use the passive voice correctly?	❏	❏
b. Did you use correct tenses?	❏	❏
5. Form		
a. Did you use correct paragraph format (indentation, division of words between syllables, margins)?	❏	❏
b. Did you use correct punctuation (capitalization, commas, periods)?		
c. Did you check the spelling of the words you are not sure of?	❏	❏

Other comments

_____

_____

_____

_____

_____

_____

_____

_____

_____

Student Name _____ Date _____

Personal reaction

_____

_____

_____

_____   _____

Chapter Checklist	<u>Good</u>	**Needs Work**
1. Content		
a. Did you support your opinion with good reasons and information?	❏	❏
b. Is your composition interesting?	❏	❏
2. Organization		
a. Do you have an introduction, supporting paragraphs, and a conclusion?	❏	❏
b. Is your focus clear?	❏	❏
c. Did you give examples to support your reasons?	❏	❏
3. Cohesion and Style		
a. Did you introduce your examples with transitions?	❏	❏
b. Did you use quotations to support your argument?	❏	❏
4. Grammar		
a. Did you use indefinite forms correctly?	❏	❏
b. Did you use *the* correctly in sentences with *of* + noun phrases?	❏	❏
5. Form		
a. Did you use correct essay form (introduction, three supporting paragraphs and a conclusion)?	❏	❏
b. Did you use correct paragraph format (indentation, division of words between syllables, margins)?	❏	❏
c. Did you use correct punctuation (capitalization, commas, periods)?	❏	❏
d. Did you check the spelling of the words you are not sure of?	❏	❏

Other comments

_____

_____

_____

_____

_____

Student Name _____ Date _____

Personal reaction

_____

_____

_____

_____

Chapter Checklist	**Good**	**Needs Work**
1. Content		
a. Is your article interesting?	❏	❏
b. Does it provide enough detail?	❏	❏
2. Organization		
a. Does your article answer the question. Who? What? Where? When? Why?	❏	❏
b. Did you have an appropriate title?	❏	❏
c. Did you include facts and not personal opinions?	❏	❏
3. Cohesion and Style		
a. Did you use restrictive relative clauses correctly?	❏	❏
b. Did you use nonrestrictive relative clauses correctly?	❏	❏
4. Grammar		
a. Did you punctuate relative clauses correctly?	❏	❏
b. Did you use correct verb tenses?	❏	❏
5. Form		
a. Did you use correct paragraph format (indentation, division of words between syllables, margins)?	❏	❏
b. Did you use correct punctuation (capitalization, commas, periods)?	❏	❏
c. Did you check the spelling of the words you not sure of?	❏	❏

Other comments

_____

_____

_____

_____

_____

_____

_____

Student Name _____ Date _____

Personal reaction

_____
_____
_____
_____

Chapter Checklist	Good	Needs Work
1. Content		
a. Did you state the problem correctly?	❏	❏
b. Did you give reasons for your proposal?	❏	❏
2. Organization		
a. Are your arguments appropriate for your audience?	❏	❏
b. Did you counter any possible objections?	❏	❏
3. Cohesion and Style		
a. Did you use the transition words for contrasting ideas correctly?	❏	❏
b. Did you use transition words for enumerating ideas correctly?	❏	❏
4. Grammar		
Did you use the conditional mood correctly?	❏	❏
5. Form		
a. Did you use correct paragraph format (indentation, division of words between syllables, margins)?	❏	❏
b. Did you use correct punctuation (capitalization, commas, periods)?	❏	❏
c. Did you check the spelling of the words you are not sure of?	❏	❏

Other comments

_____
_____
_____
_____
_____
_____
_____
_____
_____
_____